My Heritage,
My Destiny

My Heritage, My Destiny

Baiba Kreger, Ph.D.

Enjoy a life
Baiba Kreger
2014

iUniverse, Inc.

New York Bloomington Shanghai

My Heritage, My Destiny

iUniverse books may be ordered through booksellers or by contacting:

iUniverse
1663 Liberty Drive
Bloomington, IN 47403
www.iuniverse.com
1-800-Authors (1-800-288-4677)

Because of the dynamic nature of the Internet, any Web addresses or links contained in this book may have changed since publication and may no longer be valid.

The views expressed in this work are solely those of the author and do not necessarily reflect the views of the publisher, and the publisher hereby disclaims any responsibility for them.

ISBN: 978-0-595-46508-8 (pbk)
ISBN: 978-0-595-90806-6 (ebk)

Printed in the United States of America

For Tim, Jim and Melanie

Hope perches on the soul ... and sings ...
and never, never leaves.

Emily Dickenson

Contents

Foreword

There was a time, not so very long ago in America, when we saw ourselves as truly a nation of immigrants. Our culture was a cacophony of languages, customs, dress, food, faith and fun from distant lands; some familiar, others quite obscure. There was not so much a common culture as a common set of values and goals shared by new arrivals as well as those who were native born.

Most of this diverse collection of dreamers who called themselves Americans were new enough to the soil to have relatives who came through Ellis Island to make a start in this land of miracles, hope and adventure. Many still had contacts with relatives living in the "old Country," who served as reminders of rich ethnic heritages.

As the melting pot called the United States has continued to boil, the result has been more of a common culture; a sense that we are truly Americans. And as we natives drift away from the culture of our pasts, we increasingly see immigrants as threats to our language, politics, common culture and even our prosperity.

The compelling story of Baiba, Maris and the rest of the Kalnins family began at a time when America still believed the inscription on the Statue of Liberty. It began at a time when Americans willingly sacrificed their hearts, lives and treasures to rescue people from the despair of despotism; to reach out to the helpless and homeless without weighing either cost or benefit.

The Kalnins saga is truly a tale of human resilience and divine intervention. It is a testimony of the generosity of people willing to help each other even at considerable risk. It is a story of broken dreams and the courage to dream new dreams; the tenacity to make them come true.

This glimpse onto the turmoil of World War II in the Baltic states and one family's heroic struggle to not only survive, but thrive, begs to be told and needs to be remembered. We who see ourselves as "natives" ought to be reminded of the cost of freedom, paid in advance for us, by those we sometimes choose to forget. We need to be reminded of their struggles to breathe freely in this marvelous collection of peoples called the United States of America.

John Guild

Preface

A loyal understanding friend doesn't just happen. It is created. Baiba has been my friend for more years than I can remember. I see her as a survivor; she has survived the "potter's wheel" of shaping, molding, forming and repairing the cracks of adversity to and changing them to gladness.

As you read her book, you will see how God used the hardships and trials to predestine Baiba to be a strong, triumphant sojourner on the path God, in his perfect timing, caused her to follow. You will feel a part of her family and her life as she writes in a way that draws you in, to experience their suffering and pain, as well as the fun and joy of a family destined for a new life.

"When you pass through the waters, I will be with you; and when you pass through the rivers, they will not sweep over you. When you walk through the fire, you will not be burned; the flames will not set you ablaze." (Isaiah 43:2) As Baiba walked through her trials and tribulations of life, God protected her in every way. And she was always there for me when I was going through my own difficulties.

Ellen Roupp

Acknowledgments

In order to accomplish my book, I need the love and support of many people. I would like to thank the following individuals, because without their help, this book would not be possible.

First of all I would like to thank my God whose hand guided me throughout this entire project and for filling my mind with ideas and how to write them down.

Without the help of these people, my book would not be as adroit as I wanted it to be. I thank my friend John Guild for reading it and critiquing it with great suggestions; my son Tim Kreger, for his computer expertise; my son Jim and daughter Melanie for their constant support; Ellen Roupp, my very good friend and mentor who read my book with emotion; my brother, Maris Kalnins for all the invaluable information through the war and afterwards; Audrey Blobaum a good friend who read the book and gave me ideas and suggestions; Josey Gerould my friend and former neighbor who gave me a great deal of encouragement; Rasma Young for her wonderful suggestions for organizing the chapters and for the many words of encouragement. I thank all of you for your friendship and love.

Baiba Kreger

1

The Open Window

The day was beautiful and sunny on that summer morning. The front window was opened toward the street and it was low enough to the floor for a four-year-old child to stand there, listen, and let the sunrays to enter directly into the room. Flowers were blooming in a flower box just below the outside of the window. The sidewalks on either side of the street were narrow. A lonely lamppost stood in front of the house and seemed to be the only one on the street.

The skinny little blonde haired, blue-eyed girl stood at the window for a time absorbing the sounds and the sights. There seemed to be a din of noises going on in the street that would announce the morning had started and people were bustling about their business. On the narrow concrete sidewalks people chattered and scurried to the market or to their jobs.

In the distance was the all-familiar sound of horse hoofs and carriage wheels on the rumbling cobblestone streets. Then one came closer and the sound became louder until it was right in front of the window and as it passed by the window the clamoring grew dimmer and dimmer as it went on its way in the distance. The hustle and bustle on the street was a sound embedded in the four year old girl's mind. This was my home as I remember it on Rupniecibas Street, Bauska.

That child was I. It was my favorite morning pastime—to stand at the low living room window and take in the sounds of industrious people going about their business and living in a free country. It was the sound that I would not allow to leave my mind. It would become my fondest childhood memory. This was my homeland and it would soon be only a memory, my country, the land of my birth, Latvia. The sound that I had grown so accustomed to would never be again.

It was the best of times, but it was about to change. I would never again be able to recapture that sound, try as I may to lean out some window somewhere

1

else in the world. That sound is only a memory now. The morning was and still is my favorite time of the day.

Our home in Bauska was a two family, two story duplex built very sturdy with solid cement walls on each end. It belonged to my grandfather, Jakobs (Jakob) Ozols. Grandfather and his wife, Anna, had two daughters, Austra and Lucija (Lucia) and a son, Arnolds. Lucia lived on a farm near Bauska. Arnolds and Austra lived in the duplex. In better times grandfather owned and operated a weaver's shop in the front room where Arnolds now lived. It was a job he could do with one artificial leg. Jakob had his right leg amputated from an injury suffered as a soldier during WW1. Grandmother Anna died in 1938 before I was born. Grandfather remarried after Anna's death and moved to a house just outside the city of Bauska.

Everyone who lived in the duplex shared the front entrance. The open staircase led to the upstairs rooms, and a hallway went straight through to the backyard. My family lived on the left side and we occupied three rooms downstairs: kitchen; living dining bedroom rolled into one; and a big summer kitchen in the back. There were four of us; father, Arnolds; mother Laima; my brother, older by two years, Maris; and me, Baiba. The upstairs rooms were rented out to non-family persons more or less for financial reasons.

Lucia   Arnolds   Austra

There were two windows in this large room, but my favorite was the one on the right. On the wall perpendicular to the window was a large bookshelf that held encyclopedias and other books. Next to the bookshelf was a grand piano. A big flowery couch sat against the wall by the entrance to the room. This couch served as a hiding place for me whenever a stranger would come into the house. After all, I didn't want to be taken away somewhere because my behavior was not always perfect. In the middle of the room was a beautiful round mahogany table. The heating system was central in each half of the duplex house. The hearth where the logs were burned was in the big summer kitchen. The chimney was about 6 ft. square and a corner of it was in every room. White and blue tile covered the massive chimney was inside each room upstairs and down. In the winter the tiles were always warm and one could warm their hands or whatever else was cold.

My parents' bed, a majestic high headboard and a slightly lower footboard, sat in the left hand corner by the other window. My crib was pushed up against the foot of the bed. I never slept well during the night. (Sleeplessness would plague me the rest of my life.) When I awoke and everything was dark, I got very scared. I can remember being scared most of the time. Even melting snow mixed with mud was frightening to me. My way of getting comforted was to be in my parents' bed. I found that I could climb over the end of the crib and the foot of the slightly higher footboard and fall right into their bed, safe and secure once more. This seemed to work for me so I would do the same trick every night. Then my mother got an idea of how she could keep me from climbing into their bed every night. The crib was pulled back from the foot of the bed after I went to sleep. In the night, I performed the same climbing trick as all the other nights before. Once I was over the edge of the head part of the crib, I took the plunge and "ker-plunck" I hit the floor with a thud screaming, that brought both parents out of bed in an instant. Mother was pretty upset with herself and with me. I was put back into my crib but it was not moved away from the foot of the bed again. After that, I would always feel for the footboard of the bed before taking the leap!

On the right side of the house lived my father's older sister, Austra. She was a robust, energetic, but a very kind woman. Austra and Nikolais had two children, a boy, Ojars, (Oyars) the oldest of the six cousins and a girl, Mudite, (Mudeet) my brother's age. Family members of the adult kind relished in telling me that I would someday look just like Austra, skinny now and fat later.

"Why are they doing this to me," I thought. I wondered what the basis of the comparison was based on. I could not see any resemblance. If only I could have been as exceptional a person as Austra was!

Austra and Nikolais had a similar living situation as we did, with the upstairs rented out. The backyard was all fenced in and had a horse and carriage barn. It also contained the only out-house that we all used. On the right end of the house was a huge wooden gate to bring the horse and carriage inside and into to the barn. There was no running water in the house, so we hand pumped the water from the well and carried it by the pail into the house. It did not seem primitive to us because everybody got water and used toilets the same way.

When we were kids, the backyard was our playground. I remember wood piled against the wooden fence in the back. A gazebo built by my grandfather Jacobs, stood on our side of the dwelling which made a good sitting place when you were tired from running or playing hopscotch. When I first returned to Latvia in 1990, the gazebo was still standing there grown over by weeds and in a distressing condition.

The summer kitchen was used mainly for preserving or drying foods for the winter months and for doing the laundry in a big galvanized tub complete with a rubbing board.

"Let's plant some potatoes right here under the summer kitchen window," suggested Maris.

"Yes! Let's!" I replied excitedly!

In no time at all Maris had dug some holes and we dropped a potato in each one. I was most excited about making something grow, a living potato plant! The next day we eagerly went out back and dug up the potatoes to see if they had sprouted. After several days of this same procedure we finally asked Mother why the potatoes showed no progress. We told her about our care for the potatoes. She put a big smile on her face and told us that if we didn't dig the potatoes up every day, they might have a chance to sprout. After awhile we forgot all about the potatoes, but they never did sprout,+ much to my disappointment.

An older lady lived in one of the upstairs rooms on our side. We came to call her "Granny" since our paternal grandmother had died before we knew her, and our mother was an orphan at twelve. Granny from time to time was asked to keep her eye on my brother and me. Granny was in our part of the house one day to watch us. I was unhappy that my mother had gone and left us with granny. The three of us were in the kitchen. I kept on crying because **I wanted my mother**. Granny took me to the window in the kitchen and told me I had to stop crying or else.

"Baibina, do you see that man across the street walking with a sack on his back?"

"Yes," I replied gently with tears streaming down my cheeks.

"If you don't stop crying, that man is going to come in here and put you in his bag and take you away!"

"But Granny, you wouldn't let him in here would you?"

"Stop crying or I will," came the stern reply.

That did it! I ran in the living room and hid behind the couch and stayed there for a long time.

My brother was not only older than me but he was shrewd and extremely smart. When Granny was watching us again one day, she assigned my brother to watch me. I was not allowed to go out in the street and I most certainly knew it, nor did I want to go out there. The street was big scary place for me. I was apprehensive. If he saw me go out the door, he had to tell Granny right away. She promised to reward him with a chocolate bar for his laudable job. I was not aware of this deal.

"Let's go out in the street and play," Maris suggested.

"No, I'm not allowed to go out there!"

"It'll be fun. Let's go!"

"No, I don't want to! That man with the big sack on his back might come back," I protested.

Then he did the unthinkable, grabbed me by the arm and dragged me protesting out the front door. Quickly he darted back inside and locked the door. I knew I was in trouble and I realized I had been tricked. He quickly ran up the stairs to report to Granny.

"Baiba just went out the front door."

Granny would look out her upstairs window and could see the evidence with her own eyes. Maris was immediately rewarded as promised while I stood outside crying for someone to come and open the door. Maris came and let me back in and announced, "I was only playing."

This game worked for him two times, but the third time Granny became suspicious and was at her window to catch the action in progress. He did not get a chocolate bar again and did not try the game again.

The small kitchen was very simple with a tall white cupboard next to the window on the right that held everything a kitchen would need. In the right corner by the door was what seemed like a huge iron cook stove? It looked foreboding to me but provided the heat in the wintertime. Between them was a small dry sink like cupboard. In the middle of the room was a small wooden table, chairs and a high chair.

The corner by the cook stove always had a pile of wood as this was my mother's only means of cooking and she always had pans of water sitting on the stove whenever hot water was needed. This room was also our bathing room when she would fill a round galvanized tub with water from the stove.

My brother and I spent most of our time playing in the kitchen when the weather did not permit us outside. I liked playing with his horses and carriage toy and he liked playing with my tiny little brown Teddy bear.

Sometimes I would have my own bag of tricks. One day mother announced that Maris and I were going to Aunt Lucia's farm for a visit. Lucia and Ludvigs owned a farm outside of Bauska. Their two children, Skaidris (Skydris) and Zaiga, had a couple of years on Maris and I. Though it was only a few miles, it seemed like another world away in my feeble understanding of the size of the world. The horse and carriage were waiting in front of the house. I put up a fuss and didn't want to go. I felt insecure and wanted to stay with my mother. Mother gave me candy, and in tears, kicking and screaming, I was hoisted into the carriage. Away it rambled on the smooth, almost polished cobblestone street up the hill to the main road. I kept looking back as long as I could, to see if Mother was still standing there. She wasn't. With my brother beside me I felt like we were Hansel and Gretel being taken to the woods to fend for ourselves. Soon we were out of town and rolling along the open vistas of Bauska's fertile fields. This area of farmland was known as the "bread basket" of Latvia.

As it turned out, I really enjoyed the stay at the farm. I watched as the women chopped beet greens in a long wooden trough and mixed them with milled mash and water. The cows seemed to love it and slurped it up greedily. It had a tasteful aroma and looked good even for human consumption, I thought. Almost the same kind of slop was prepared for the pigs. The two women would pick up the wooden trough by rope handles on each end and place it in the pen for the pigs. Immediately the ten or so piglets would run to the trough. Noisily grunting, some standing with all fours in the trough, they slurped the wonderful meal. Sometimes I was allowed to try chopping the greens with the sharp spade like tool, which was two times my height. My brother, on the other hand, went to the fields and worked with the men. He was close to the age of his tow headed cousin, Skydris. Both young lads ran, played and did their work as young boys could. Little did either one of them realize what the world would hold for them.

At the farm, my brother discovered the beehives. No, he couldn't just watch the bees at work flying in and out; he had to see what they would do if he annoyed them just a little! As he tried blocking their entry with a piece of glass, he found out that the bees get very angry and he would need to run like hell to get away from them, swatting the stingers as he fled his own folly. Consequences did not seem to scare him much!

The chickens ran about the farm freely. I found it to be very entertaining to throw oats out by the handfuls and watch them come running to peck the grain.

Their plump little bodies were swayed this way and that as they ran. The rooster always came to alert the hens of the newly fallen oats, scratching the ground as if he single-handedly had found the gold mine. Now that the hens were so close and in my control, I decided it was time I should pick up one of these adorable feathered creatures. The hens, of course, had other ideas. And so the chase was on. I liked this game of power over the hens because a hen will squat and lower her wings to the ground in surrender rather quickly.

While I was enjoying my game of "empress of the hens," Aunt Lucia was not. Chasing the hens would make them quit laying and the rooster might attack me … what was I thinking? Much to the amusement of my brother, I was reprimanded and sent to the house. Okay.

What to do? The farmhouse kitchen was quite small, had a free standing cabinet, a small table and the ever-present cook stove. All of the cooking was done on the wood-fired stove—summer and winter. The dinning room was larger and had a huge table in the middle covered with a lace tablecloth. A hutch stood against one wall and was also covered with a white lace cloth. On the hutch I spied it, a clear glass rabbit about 12 inches long, which gave the appearance of a slightly tinted green color. This marked the beginning of my love affair with rabbits!

I took that glass rabbit and placed it on the table and pretended to walk it all around the edge of the table, letting it nibble on the clover that grew in my imagination on the lace tablecloth. This was even better than trying to catch chickens! So engrossed was I in my rabbit game that I never saw or heard the dinning room door open. There was Aunt Lucia.

"I'm just playing with this rabbit. He is so beautiful. Can I take him home?"

"No, no, and no, the rabbit is not a toy. You can look at him but you cannot carry him around because you could drop him and he will break. Let me put it back on the hutch," she scolded.

As soon as Lucia left, I took the rabbit back to the table and continued my fantasy. Some time later Lucia came back in. Busted! This time the rabbit was put up on a high shelf and my fun-time was over. "Why won't Aunt Lucia let me have any fun?" I wondered. I like hens and I only wanted to hold some of them and pet them. And how could I possibly hurt a glass rabbit!

When it was time to go home from my aunt's farm, I didn't want to leave. I put up a big fuss. I was not leaving without that glass rabbit. My brother was already seated in the carriage but I was wailing, crying and would not get in the carriage. Not wanting to drive into town with a screaming three-year old, Aunt Lucia said she would go get the rabbit so I could take it home. I immediately stopped my protest and waited with arms outstretched as she brought the rabbit out. She said that he would be safer in the back of the carriage where it was placed under a blanket. We were finally off with Lucia at the reins.

Once back in town and as soon as I was lifted out of the carriage, I promptly hurried to the back of the carriage to get my rabbit. Aunt Lucia lifted the blanket and said the glass rabbit was gone!

"Where's the rabbit?" I asked looking worried.

"It must have fallen out on our way here and is lost. See, we should have left it in the dining room where he would be safe. If you hadn't insisted that the rabbit be brought along, we would still have it. Now it is gone," she scolded. Even then, in my three-year-old wisdom, I knew that an adult was lying to me. I never got the chance to go back to the farm to see if the rabbit was still there. In my mind I knew it was.

Before I was two years of age, I was a normal chubby baby. I was dressed with the high-topped leather shoes, the cotton dresses that were past my knees, complete with a white pinafore. With very thin light blond hair and bluish-gray eyes, what's not to love?

Then it struck! A killing disease called diphtheria. In 1940, there was no penicillin in Latvia or any other miracle drugs. I was sent to a children's hospital and spent months being nursed back to health with doses of very hot milk and spoonfuls of honey. Frightened and alone, I cried a lot. I can vividly remember the nurses at the hospital in their crisp white garb coming with the spoonfuls of the home remedy forcing it down my tightening throat. And I remember sitting at the cafeteria table with the other children, but not touching any food. From then on nothing tasted good and I could eat very little. Mother said I looked like a shoestring when I finally came home, the skinny condition that would remain with me until I was thirty-two.

Most people back then did not survive this dreaded disease, but for some reason God had spared my life.

Baiba at age one in Jelgava

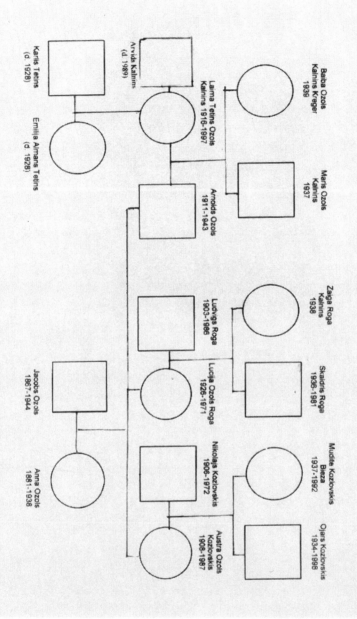

OZOLS FAMILY TREE

2

The Head Forester

The First World War started in 1914. Two years into the war, Emilija (Emilia) and Karlis Tetins had taken refuge in Vitebsk, Russia. The people of Bauska were evacuated because of the war. While in Vitebsk, on August 24, 1916 Emilia delivered their second child, a girl, they named Laima. The name meant good fortune or luck. Their first child, Irene, was born several years earlier but died of complications of pneumonia as a toddler. So, Laima was definitely the "good fortune" they had longed for and welcomed into their empty lives. After all, they were safe from the war and they had a gift from heaven.

The collapse of the German and Russian empires in WW1 allowed Latvia, Lithuania and Estonia to become free independent states. Soon afterwards, the Tetins family returned to Bauska. Bolshevik Revolution ended the Czarist rule in Russia and the Latvians established a new government. Latvia was declared a liberated and sovereign nation, a free independent Latvia on November 18, 1918. After 700 years of foreign rule, Latvia was at last free! Even though the Latvian army could not beat the mighty Russian or German armies, they fought valiantly and from one such battle generated the Latvian flag. A mortally wounded solder had been covered with a white sheet on the battlefield and had bled so badly that only a narrow strip in the middle of the sheet remained white. The two outside edges had turned a garnet red.

The Russians signed a peace treaty with Latvia, never to invade our land again by force. The Latvians elected a prime minister, Karlis Ulmanis, who later became the first Latvian president. Independence Day was celebrated with solemn ceremonies, national costumes, folk music and dancing on November 18, 1918 and still is today. Latvians enjoyed twenty years of freedom and self-rule. People prospered. There was peace. Welfare did not exist, but socialized medicine was available to anyone in the country.

The expropriated forests became government property and became a valuable source of exports for Latvia. Karlis Tetins was appointed Head Forester in the

Bauska vicinity and worked for the Latvian government. He was in charge of what trees were to be cut, when they would be cut and how much a man would be charged for the timbers. Then the timber was transported to saw mills to be cut into lumber.

Karlis had an office in the house that was designated for the forester, but owned by the government. The property was located in the country close to the national forests. It had enough land to be a self-sufficient farm. There were cows, pigs, chickens, ducks, geese, goats, and of course horses for transportation needs. People came to his office to buy timber and firewood. Although he worked for a salary, his job was very important and along with it came a lot of responsibility. The forests could not be depleted, so with careful planning the timber would regenerate. And that was Karlis' job.

Emilia took charge of the household duties. She had a large crew to cook for each day. There were the workers to tend the crops, the animals, and the large garden; the men who worked in the woods; and the household servants. Usually about 12–15 people graced Emilia's huge dinning room table. Every day she would do all the cooking and baking on the wood-fired kitchen cook stove, summer or winter. It was meat, potatoes and gravy for the hearty appetites. All of the meat was farm raised and very fresh. The vegetables came from the garden and were kept in a dirt cellar that stayed cool in the summer and kept well over the winter too. Every week she would bake the course very dark rye bread—a Latvian specialty! Everyone at the Tetins household worked very hard and the meals were only part of their pay. This was a job Emilia enjoyed to the fullest with little Laima growing up in a very happy household.

The house was quite large and very plain, yet it had all the amenities a farmhouse needed. It was equipped with a large kitchen, laundry room (all the water had to be carried in by pails), a large dinning room, a sauna, and several small bedrooms. Bedrooms were usually small since people did not spend much time in them except to sleep. The extra bedrooms were for the hired help. As with other homes, there was no indoor bathroom, only an outhouse. Like most homes out in the country, the Tetins house was a wooden structure with wood shingles and horizontal boards for siding. The home was not designed for its architectural beauty, but for function and comfort.

Laima had an ideal life on the farm near the edge of The Dirda National Forest. Her parents loved and spoiled her very much. Anything she wanted, they did for her. She had a tutor that came to the house every day because it was too far for a very young girl to get to school in town. As she got a little older, she decided to go to the town and attend public school. Karlis would take her in horse and buggy. In one spot the river was quite shallow, and Karlis would take the horse and buggy through the water instead of going all the way to the bridge. When the horses didn't want to go through the water, Karlis would gently encourage them. They trusted him. In warmer weather, she would walk along the Musa River to the bridge that would take her into town. Countless times she walked along the path of the river. In the coldest part of the winter, the Musa would freeze over so hard that horse and sleigh could cross it easily and quickly.

At age twelve, Laima's beautiful world began to crumble. Karlis suffered a fatal heart attack, and within six months her mother was dead from cancer of the lymph nodes. She had buried both of her parents in the Bauska Cemetery. Latvian's have many "dainas" or poetic sayings, and this one reminded Laima of her dear mother:

> *Light the fire, light the candle.*
> *How dark is my room?*
> *But mother enters in,*
> *And suddenly, the room turns bright!*

When I returned to Bauska 45 years later, my mission was to find their graves. I looked at the map of the cemetery, which mother had sketched, but the exact place where the graves should be could not be located. The spot where it should have been was a fresh grave that had a new stone engraved with a Russian name. All records of the cemetery had been sent to Moscow and were not available. Putting the facts together, Oyars and I decided that where their graves should be, another body was buried on top of them or worse yet, their remains had been destroyed. My mother takes another devastating blow from the Russians. Nothing is sacred to the "Ruskies", no, not even the dead!

Laima was now an orphan. The year was 1928 and already there were rumors of unrest in Europe and Russia. She had no one. No aunts, no uncles, no one at all. She was all-alone in a world that had no mercy for her. She was sent to Riga, the capital city of Latvia, to live with a distant cousin. She attended a much larger school, but living the easy life that she had with her parents, she was not happy in Riga. The young cousin tried to make her comfortable and help her adjust, but to a 12 year-old girl everything was so strange and large and different. She hated every minute she spent in Riga. She wanted to return to Bauska, where at least things were familiar. A very good friend of Emilia's, Mrs. Draudzins, invited Laima to come and live with her. She had only been in Riga a couple of weeks and was delighted to be back in Bauska.

Mrs. Draudzins had only one child, a son named Ossi. He was equally as spoiled as Laima. He wanted a motorcycle bad enough that his father bought him one much to the dismay of Ossi's mother. He drove the cycle way too fast and ripped around the yard and woods with it. His mother fretted and worried that he would get hurt or maimed or worse. Then it happened! One day Ossi hit a tree with the cycle. Even though he wasn't seriously hurt, Mrs. Draudzins decided enough was enough! While her husband was at work and Ossi in school, she dug a big hole in the ground behind the shed and buried that sucker! End of motorcycle woes.

Laima referred to Ossi as her brother, but always explained that he wasn't, really. Ossi was very bright. His grades in school were excellent. Ossi would one day reach the United States too and graduate from college with a degree in art. A talented man, he was a sculptor and a painter. He lived in Chicago with his very beautiful wife, Milda. Ossi built the house himself and had made a big back yard, full of all kinds of plants and trees. My mother would only get to see him one time since the escape from Latvia, when Mother and I took a trip out west in 1976. We stopped in Chicago for a visit. Ossi invited us in and showed us his beautiful house and his collection of swords and his paintings. He drove us around Chicago to show us some of his sculptures and some that he was in charge of restoring one of which was the famous horse and rider statue near the fountain.

The dinner his wife put on for us was not only delicious, but very interesting. Ossi had a plain run of the mill ally cat, a tiger. As we were eating from the beautiful bone china dishes and fine stemware, Ossi mentioned that he doesn't own the house but the cat does. But the cat allows them to live there.

About that time the cat jumped on the table and walked around every dish and sniffed it. I thought my mother would have a conniption! She doesn't even allow cats in the house let alone on the table! But she never said a word.

Then Ossi said, "Tiger will walk around the table, but he will never eat anything. He just checks everything to make sure it is all right for us. Before we left to go back on the Amtrak, for our treck home, Mother asked him for one of his paintings. She never got it. When Ossi died, Mother found out about it in the Latvian newspaper LAIKS, meaning TIME.

Baby Laima at age one

3

The Window Closes

I was born in a town called Jelgava, on March 18, 1939, not too far from Bauska. My father had finished his law degree at the University of Riga and was practicing law in Jelgava when I was born. Those was peaceful times. Latvia had enjoyed twenty years of sovereignty as a nation free from occupation of larger stronger countries. When the judge left Jelgava, my father was appointed the new judge. Life was very promising for a young couple and two children. I was baptized in a Lutheran church in Jelgava as my brother had been two years earlier. It was then that I became a child of God. The Lutheran church would play an important role in my life.

First the rumors of war came and then the war. On January 30, 1939, Hitler threatened the Jews in a speech. His words about the Jews echoed the beginning of WWII. In March Hitler invaded and took Czechoslovakia. A few days later, Nazis signed a "Pact of Steel" with Italy, the forerunner of the Axis power. On August 23, 1939, Hitler and Stalin signed a non-aggression treaty, also known as the Molotov-Ribbentrop Treaty. The secret protocols defined the territorial divisions that Nazi Germany and the Soviets would take after Hitler's invasion of Poland on September 1, 1939. The Soviets then invaded Eastern Poland. On October 8, 1939 the Baltic States were compelled to sign mutual assistance treaties. When Finland refused, it was attacked by the Soviets. In June of 1940, Soviets invaded Latvia and annexed the country by August 5, 1940. The scene was similar of what happened in Estonia and Lithuania. By July 1940, the Soviets occupied all three Baltic States. Once more Latvia was under siege of a bigger power, Russia. The Russians came in with garrisons of troops that exceeded Latvia's peacetime armies. No more law, lawyers or judges. Pandemonium was the order of the day. No more freedom. No more good life. Then in 1941 the war took a strange turn when the Nazis beat the Soviets back to Leningrad and Germans occupied the country of Latvia.

My family moved back to Bauska so my father could take a job in a grocery store as an accountant. We moved into the Ozols' duplex on Rupniecibas Street #13.

I thought my world was still perfect. I had a mother and a father. We lived in a nice place. I enjoyed the sunshine and the grass; the white clover and colorful flowers. And in the winter, I had warm clothing to bundle up, as there was always an abundance of snow.

A horse and carriage would take us wherever we needed to go, and of course in winter, the horse and sleigh. "The world was in order," thought my small mind.

In warmer weather we would go on walking excursions. Two rivers flowed into Bauska, our hometown, Memele and Musa. Between the rivers stood a castle ruin high into the sky. The rivers served as the moat for the castle that once housed the feudal Lords of German decent, who in the Middle Ages ruled the small vicinity. Built of some very crude red bricks, most of the castle was in ruin and was open to the atmosphere. Hundreds of years ago it was a fortress for the aristocracy. Now kids could play among the crumbling walls and people could climb up to the higher places and see across Bauska. My brother and I played hide-and-go seek while the adults sat on the park benches and talked about the war.

The world was in turmoil by 1943. The Battle of Britton was raging; the Nazis sank 27 merchant ships in the Atlantic and were advancing in every direction in Europe; Japan bombed Pearl Harbor on Dec. 7, 1941; and the Americans had entered WWII. Much, much more was going on in Europe, but it is too numerous to account for in this story. I knew nothing about any war.

Then there came a numbing sadness. My mind was intensely troubled because something was very, very wrong, and way too wrong for a four-year-old to understand. I could only look out the window and wonder. What was happening, why the gloom? The window was closed now. The tears slowly rolled down my cheeks but still I stood at the window, my mind as far away as it could be at that age. There was no one to comfort me or hold me. Feeling alone again, I thought about Mother and wondered if she was crying too and I wanted to be with her. My brother had gone with Mother to the burial, but I was left with a sitter. Because the weather was bad, Mother thought it was best that I stay at home, trying to protect my health. Then there was talk of a funeral, but I had no clue what that word meant. I don't really know when I understood that my father had died. He became ill and was taken to Riga, the capital city, to the hospital. The diagnosis was not good. It was TB and it was the fast spreading kind, diffusing through both lungs. His lungs were full of the disease and he would live less than four weeks. It was May 26, 1943. He was 32 years old. He had accomplished a lot in his short 32 years, but death took its grip and he was gone. He was buried in the Bauska Cemetery and had a large tall monument put at his grave. His father, Jakobs with quivering chin remarked at the burial, "My dear son, your death is my fault." My life would change forever.

When I went back to Latvia in 1990, Oyars took me to the cemetery and showed where the grave was once. It is no more. The Russians had destroyed it and there was no trace of the monument either. Not even the dead are sacred with the Communist barbarians!

Again I stood at my window, but still it was closed. It was raining again and I watched the raindrops fall on the glass pane and run down to disappear forever. "What was the race to vanish so fast? Where would each of these droplets of water end up? Where was my father now?" These things I pondered but kept in my heart.

I remember my father only as a very tall, thin figure. When he would come home in the evening, I ran into his open arms and he lifted me up way over his head and then would twirl around in circles. I was scared to be that high, but begged for more each day. Then the most fun of all was when he let me put my little feet on his shiny black shoes and walk back and forth while he hung on to my hands. Oh what fun! Those would be my only recollections of my father, and the fondest in my childhood. I could not remember an image of his face though. In my mind he was only this tall figure, fun loving, always in a suit; the only impression I had of a man without a face. I would not see an image of his face until 45 years later.

When my father was still alive, Mother used to finish his coffee in the morning after he left for work. Mother was never one to waste anything. The fatal tuberculin bacteria was now also in her body. She was taken to a sanatorium and we were left with a sitter. Another separation, complicated with the fear of never seeing my mother again, my perfect world was crumbling fast. My brother was also admitted for observation of the same disease. He was released without any symptoms. Mother would later admit to me that her survival was due to her stubborn will to live and because she forced herself to eat the oatmeal that was brought to her every day. It would keep her from losing more weight and would eventually help to regain her health and return home.

Mother, now in her mid-twenties, was a widow with two small children, a tuberculosis survivor and the war was very intense in Europe. Without any means of support, Mother took a job at the local bank in Bauska. My brother and I were taken to a kindergarten type of day care. I hated it, and cried everyday, but to no avail.

Then a horticulturist, Arvids Kalnins, entered into my mother's life. Arvids, a handsome young man, operated a greenhouse business with his Mother, Charlotte, growing and marketing roses and fresh vegetables year round. Arvids was the younger of Charlotte's two boys, Robert and Arvids. The business was located in the center of Bauska on the main street, Uzvara. They rented more greenhouses in another part of town to meet the demands of the business. I know little of Arvids' father since he had died long before. Both brothers were avid sportsmen, playing soccer, volleyball, skiing and swimming. Their best friend, Rudy, completed the trio of comradeship that would last a lifetime. Little did the comrades know that sports would be in their past forever. Little did Arvids know that the unfortunate soccer accident would end up saving his life? Arvids was spared from the army because of a broken leg from a soccer accident. The leg had not been set right and it sort of bowed inward from his knee to his ankle. Physically, the leg was a handicap and he would never participate in any sport again. Rudy's destiny would very closely hinge on Arvids and his new family.

Born Rudolfs Putenis, he was soon nicknamed Rudy. He was very athletic and in great health. He was just barely out of high school, but had no family. His parents had died and he had no siblings. One thing about Rudy is that he was always happy and smiling and joking. Rudy's and Arvids' favorite sports were volleyball and soccer. And they were very good at it. Rudy was very handsome and had a lot of appeal for the young ladies. Later in Germany he had a beautiful Latvian girlfriend, named Regina. She was as nice as she was pretty. They made a perfect couple. Regina moved to Canada with her mother and a life with Rudy would not be their destiny. But when he got to America, he married a woman named Valda, not a great beauty but a good partner in life. They had two children, a girl, Andra and a boy, Martins. Rudy lived the rest of his life working in a factory in New Jersey until his retirement. He died in 1999. His wife still lives in New Jersey.

It was summertime and we would go down to the river Musa. Sometimes we swam and sometimes just soaked up the wonderful sunrays, Arvids, Laima and us and often Rudy. The shoreline was like a carpet of soft mowed grass, not kept with mowers but from grazing animals. Sometimes the carpet was interspersed with patches of warm, white sand. In the water grew rushes and other water plants. The water was very clear and clean. Laima liked to walk on the smooth white stones beneath the water that seemed to form a path along the river. On quiet evenings, we could hear something that sounded like thunder. Thunder it wasn't, but cannons it was! It sounded as though the front line was not far off, perhaps in Lithuania, just five kilometers south of Bauska.

In 1942 the Germans occupied Latvia. Robert, drafted into the German army was already stationed in Germany. Robert's wife, Millie, was still in Tukums with her daughter, Biruta (Tuta for short). Robert, taller than his younger brother, enjoyed fraternizing with his buddies and friends. One could find him playing cards; smoking cigarettes; having powerful discussions; and indulging in the spirits several nights a week. Millie did not seem to mind or at least never said anything about it.

Robert was an extremely bright man. He earned two PhD's in agricultural science at the University of Riga, but because of the war, he never got to apply his knowledge in Latvia. He would later earn his third PhD in the same field in the USA.

"Maybe we should go and visit my sister-in-law, Millie, for awhile," Arvids suggested. "She is alone with her teenage daughter now, and we should check on her." Besides that, she lived in Tukums, which is north west of us and much farther away from Lithuania. The war situation being so close was of grave concern and anything could change very quickly any day. So going to Millie's was a comforting idea for the time being. We did not realize at the time that the decision to visit Millie was our destiny that would take us to far ends of the world. The cannon sounds grew closer and closer each day.

Mother worked in a Bauska bank and had two weeks vacation coming. Arvids had greenhouses to take care of, but in the middle of the summer he could leave one of his workers in charge and not worry. A few days before Mother's vacation began; they could see troop movement in town. German soldiers had stopped at the market place to get food and to drink from the well. Some of the bank workers had stepped outside the bank building and were surveying the arrival of the soldiers and what it might mean to all of us.

"We geht es?" ("How are things going for you?") inquired one of the soldiers looking at Alvina who was standing on the bank steps.

"Only God knows and only He can help," came a reply from one of the older soldiers in the group, as he looked up into the sky before Alvina had a chance to answer.

It was July 27, 1944; Mother was at work all day. We would leave for Millie's the next day. How we would get there was not clear yet, but probably we would take the bus that left Bauska three times a day. But going by bus had a disadvantage since we could take very little with us. For a two-week stay that did not sound auspicious. Laima returned home from the bank at 4:30 PM. to Arvids's exciting announcement—that he had made arrangements with a man to take us to Tukums in a truck. But we must be ready in a few hours. We had to get everything packed tonight as the truck was leaving very early the next morning at daybreak. "And pack food to take along," added Arvids. Then he left for his garden house to pack some of his own things.

Arvids later explained how he was able to arrange for the truck. On the street he had met man he knew as Mr. Kalnitis, the owner of the truck. He was carrying a truck part that needed to be fixed and asked Arvids if he knew how to fix it. Mr. Kalnitis said he had arranged to take many families to Kurzeme, a western county in Latvia. It was in the same direction as Tukums, a small city. The trip is slated for tomorrow and now I can't find anyone to fix this part. It sure sounds like destiny.

"I know somebody who has a garage and can fix that for you before tomorrow, but you have to promise to take my family along. We want to go to Tukums," Arvids stated.

"It's a deal!" replied Kalnitis much relieved about his predicament.

Arvids took Kalnitis to see Mr. Jekobson and the truck part was fixed. Kalnitis, of course, kept his promise and we were leaving to visit Aunt Millie in the morning. Now that we were going on a truck, a lot more things could be taken along. The cannon sounds seemed closer each day.

Arvids had been trading fresh vegetables, most importantly cabbage, from his greenhouses with the government and received rationing coupons. The only way a person could buy certain items was with these coupons (during the German occupation). The rationed items included sugar, cigarettes, coffee and liquor. Since the coupons needed to be used by a certain time, you had to purchase things you didn't need or want or you would lose them. Mother bought mostly sugar, but when that was not available, then cigarettes and liquor. She thought they might be handy not for our own use but as barter. It certainly turned out to be the case.

It was like Mother had had a premonition or was one to store up and be prepared for anything. The summer of 1944, while Germans were retreating from the Allied forces, she made jams and preserves with the rationed sugar and packed the jars in a wooden box cushioned with straw, thinking that if we had to leave in a hurry, these would be ready to go. Arvids' Mother had given Mother some heavy linen dishtowels. Mother sewed them into small sacks and filled the sacks with what sugar she had left. These are the items she first thought of to take along to Millie's.

Then some clothing decisions had to be made. It was summer, so not much thought was given to warm clothing for winter. In two weeks we would be back anyway! I was at the chest of drawers deciding what I should take along, trying to convince Mother to let me take some red and white striped cotton stockings along because, "I like them so much." The answer was a stern NO, because it was summer and it was too hot to wear them anyway. They would be useless. Then Mother removed some pictures from photo albums and threw them in the trunk along with some books. She packed bottles of liquor in a suitcase, also cushioned with straw.

That evening Arvids arrived with a horse and carriage to take our belongings and put them on the truck. His Mother had added a few things too—a chest, a Singer Sewing machine (hand crank), and food to include her own made rye bread and a huge smoked ham. Charlotte would join us in a few days at Millie's house in Tukums. She thought she would take the bus.

When everything was on the truck Arvids took all of us to his garden house to spend the night as he thought it would be safer not to be right in town. The rumors were spreading that the Russians might bomb Bauska during the night. Needless to say, none of us slept much that night.

Arnolds Ozols

Laima Tetins

N. BALGALVIS, FOTO-STUD. RĪGĀ

Arnolds and Laima
Feb. 14, 1937

Austra, Grandma Anna, Arnolds, Lucia

Grandfather Jakops Ozols

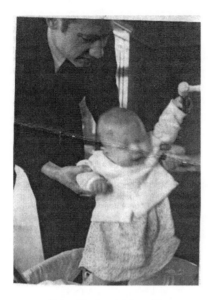

Baby Maris and Arnolds

Maris' Christening
Aunt Lucia and Uncle Nicolais
Godparents

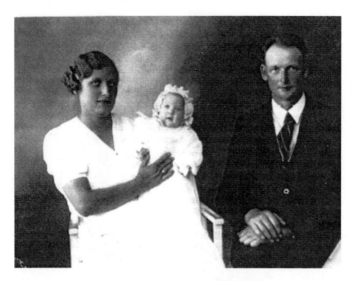

Baiba's Christening
Aunt Austra and Uncle Ludvigs
Godparents

4

On the Way to Millie's House

At Arvids' garden house the flowers were in blossom, not to mention an entire field of white roses. Arvids picked a bouquet of the roses and gave them to Laima just before going to the truck. With roses in arm and two children in tow, we arrived at the truck.

Many other families were already gathered with their belongings. The truck was loaded completely full with boxes, trunks and suitcases. All of us had to get on top of the load for the ride, 16 people in all. Charlotte had come along to see us off. She was very concerned about our safety on top of the load. Any one of us could easily fall off. She must have had something like this in mind before we left the garden house. In no time at all, she had a new white rope secured several times across the top of the load so we could all hang on to it for safety. She would come to Millie's in a day or two. She needed to get somebody to care for the animals while she was gone and she would take the horse and wagon to Millie's. Arvids would never see his Mother again.

Mr. Kalnitis wanted to cross the Musa River at the crack of dawn just in case the German soldiers try to confiscate the truck. We were heading northwest toward Jelgava, then to Tukums. At the bridge over Musa were guards. Would we get through? They turned out to be our own Latvian soldiers and none of them asked questions or tried to flag us down. Whew!

About two kilometers farther, we were stopped by some civilians who gave us the news that the Russians had already crossed the Lithuanian border and were on the main road north of us, the exact direction we were heading. They told us that Jelgava was burning and had been evacuated. All of the families begged the driver to go back to Bauska and started pounding on the roof of the cab. He finally turned the truck around and we went back across the Musa River and wove through the town center; then across the Memele River to the main highway, north to Riga. It was still early in the morning and people were not stirring yet. The town was quiet. As the truck continued its journey, the adult travelers had taken notice that the roadside was marked where mines had been placed. The truck drove on and on.

On the highway to Riga, a Russian soldier was walking along the road. He flagged down the truck, was lost and asked for information regarding Russian troop movements. Of course, none of us knew anything about the Russian troops! Mother asked him if he had eaten lately then gave him a sandwich. We continued on our way. Before the Riga city limits, Mr. Kalnitis decided to turn off the main highway and use a smaller road that he was familiar with, to get to Tukums. With the exception of a few patrolmen on motorcycles, we saw very little traffic. Only one of them stopped us to ask if we had seen any Russian tanks. Thank God we had not!

Just a few kilometers from Tukums we encountered a road block of German soldiers with cannons. They asked the driver who we were.

"We are protected families being evacuated," declared Mr. Kalnitis.

"Let the women and children go," shouted one of the soldiers, "the men should stay and fight to hold back the oncoming Russian troops!"

Mother was amused at the thought that this little group could possibly hold back Russian tanks, but was full of fear that we would not be allowed to go through. My brother was sitting a little farther away, but I was huddled close to Mother and we did not move our heads to look around. Then a senior German officer came around to our side of the truck and stopped right in front of us. He seemed to be in charge. He stared straight into our faces. Mother and I froze for a time with fear! He looked at us for a brief moment, what seemed to be an eternity for us, and then raised his arm to motion to his soldiers to let us pass. It could only be God's intervention in this officer's mind to let us go on.

"I will never forget that man's face as long as I live," Mother would tell us years later. "And he was a German!" It was only the first time that Germans would come to our aid.

The truck continued on to Tukums. We did not eat that day or make stops for bathroom purposes. I could not hold my bladder any longer, nor was I about to complain about my needs, so I let it go and peed all over the baggage and boxes where I was sitting. I had lost one of my shoes when my foot became lodged between boxes. I was very upset from being wet and losing my shoe. I shed some quiet tears but made no sound. Until the truck was unloaded, I walked around with one shoe and urine soaked clothing.

Tukums was bustling with activity. People were leaving. The town was being evacuated! Arvids ran to Millie's house but found out that Millie and her daughter, Biruta, nicknamed Tuta had already left that morning. The Russian tanks were close to Tukums. Jelgava was burning. How can we stay here? What would we do now?

Our belongings are still on the truck. Mr. Kalnitis said to stay on and ride to the Ugal train station, which was his destination. From then on it was destiny for us. We would take it one day, one moment at a time. The truck arrived at the Ugal station in the evening. For most of the families, this was the final stop. Arvid paid Mr. Kalnitis 1000 marks, which covered some of the other passengers also.

One of the women on the truck with us was Mrs. Jankovskis, whose brother just happened to be the director of the Ugal station. He took all of us to his home that night. Yes, all 16 of us. That night we slept on the floor on a carpet all in a row like sardines. It was a roof over our heads, at least for one night. The big question was not what we would eat, but where would we go from here?

Mr. Kalnitis departed in the morning. We never heard from him or about him again. Mrs. Jankovskis's intention was to live with her Mother and sister just a few kilometers from Ugal, on a farm near Piltene. She invited our family to come and stay with them. Arvid thought that going to a farm was a good idea because there would be something to eat, at least milk, butter, eggs and bread. Arvid accepted the invitation. After it was all said and done Mrs. Jankovskis had asked other people to come and stay at the farm too. Together there were 11 people to go to the farm. Mrs. Jankovskis's brother-in-law came with 2 horses and 2 wagons to transport all of us to the farm.

We had our own room at the farm and our food that we brought along. There were fields of crops, vegetable and flower gardens. The River Venta was not far away for swimming and sunning. It would have been a decent place to stay except that we knew nothing of what was going on in the world. There was no newspaper, no radio and of course, no TV. Rumors had it that the Russians were in Tukums. They had closed all of the main roads and shut down the railroads. There wasn't much hope that Charlotte would make it to Tukums. How much longer would it be before the Russians came further? This was the even bigger question!

Then new rumors came to Piltene, this time that the Russians had been driven out of Tukums by German and Latvian forces and that the roads were open again and maybe even the railroads. Arvids' hope was renewed that his Mother might be able to travel to Tukums after all. It was only a hope. We had no way of knowing, where Charlotte was, but we saw many refugees come through every day. Laima quickly sent a letter off to Tukums hoping that Millie's Mother would get it or that the mail system was even operating. Remarkably, Laima received a letter back about three weeks later from Millie's cousin, Mirza who was still in

Tukums. The letter explained that Millie and Tuta had left Tukums on July 28 (the same day we left Bauska) in an army truck traveling to Germany. Millie's Mother had not gone along, but had received a letter from Millie who by now was living in Heidelberg. At that time the roads to Germany were still open to travel. Mirza included the address where Millie was staying. As we look back on the happenings, we can see how God was lining up his plan for us. It was His destiny for us.

One of the refugee families who were with us on the truck and now living at the farm were named Gize. Their family had been prepared to leave by boat for Sweden. The boat was docked on the Venta River, but to reach the Baltic Sea the boat would have to go to Ventspils, one of the seaports. At the seaport, they needed a special permit because everything was under guard. Shortly after, the Gize family moved to a schoolhouse, where other refugee families were staying, to await the permit to sail.

By this time the general mobilization had started. Every able man was to report to the area draft board. Mr. Gize and Arvids both were notified to appear in Ventspils in a couple of days. This was one of the most dreaded days Mother had feared, because they were taking almost everybody into the army. It meant that she and her children would be left by themselves at the farm. The best she could hope for was to earn her keep at the farm and do what work she could.

Mother cried and cried and prayed and prayed. Then she went to the train station to see Arvids off. She didn't know if it might be the last time she would ever see him. God's hand intervened again. Destiny. Arvids had been examined by a Latvian doctor, who deemed that Arvids' leg was not yet healed and because it was not set properly, looked terribly crooked. The doctor made the decision that Arvids' health was not fit to go into the army and his leg needed more healing time. What an unexpected blessing this was for Laima! She thanked God for answering her prayers. It meant that we could stay together. It was the most wonderful news.

Mr. Gize was drafted and was given a time and place to report for duty in the German army. He had to do something fast so he could stay together with his family. By this time the permit to cross the Baltic Sea had come through. The Gize family and his sister's family prepared to leave Latvia. They were seven people in all. The boat was quite small. Mr. Gize had offered for us to come along, but that would make 11 people on the open boat, so that idea was dropped. It was too risky. We did not hear from them again. At the same time Arvids toyed with the idea of going back to Bauska to look for his mother before doing anything else. When he got news that all citizens had been evacuated from Bauska and all roads were closed, he gave up on that idea too. It was September already and Riga had fallen to the Russians.

When the Gize family left, we moved to the schoolhouse and took the room they had occupied. All this time we did not know what we would do or where we would go next. We had no means of transportation except to walk everywhere. Even if we walked, we could not take our belongings with us as they were too big and heavy to carry. If the trains were running, we could get someplace, but where? There was talk that people could go by boat to Germany from Ventspils and Liepaja (Liepaya), the two western seaports in Latvia. When the Russians had taken Riga, they also took control of Madones radio station. Every day the Russians were warning that people should not get on the German boats because they would be bombed and sunk. Russians were also reporting that many boats had already been sunk. Some civilians were pulled out of the water by the Baltic Sea Coast Guard or their bodies had simply washed ashore. What to believe? What to do? Where to go? Arvids thought that going to Germany was not a good idea because of the air raids and bombing.

The schoolhouse became overcrowded with Russian refugee families. No one knew where they came from or why they were in Latvia. The schoolhouse ran out of water from overuse. Not a drop! We had to then walk to a small stream, quite a distance away, and carry the water back in cans. Mother had baked some bread and dried the slices so we had something to eat when we traveled again. Arvids and Maris would go fishing at the nearby river, but only by night so nobody would see them. These fish were dried, probably by the sun dried method to eat later.

The woman custodian at the schoolhouse was very kind to us. She told us about a friend who had a farm near a great forest. Arvids and Mother walked to the farm and were warmly greeted by the owner, a middle aged woman who was trying to run the farm by herself with two other women, one of them elderly. She sincerely wanted us to come and live at the farm. "If the Russians come here, we can all run into the woods," she told them and then added, "Out of the woods come deserters and Russians who are hiding by day and asking for food by night."

"I give food to everyone who comes and asks," she continued. The nature of this announcement troubled Arvids. He and Mother decided that it was not a good idea to live there and walked back to the schoolhouse.

Arvids had a friend, from college days at The Buldure School of Horticulture. His mother owned a farm on the other side of the Venta River. Arvids knew the address. The schoolhouse custodian agreed to watch my brother and me, and then the two started on foot to the Salts' farm. The road was filled with horses and wagons that had traveled from the eastern part of Latvia, called Vidzeme. The setting reminded my Mother of some movies she had watched with scenes of covered wagons. The only way to cross the Venta River was by ferry, and the ferry could only take a few horses and wagons across at a time. The line waiting to cross the river was very long; horses, wagons and people on foot. While Arvids and Mother were waiting their turn, they talked to a farmer who had come from Vidzeme.

"What do you think one should do, go to Germany or stay here in Latvia on a farm?" asked Arvids.

"My son is in the army and was ordered to stay where the Russians had already invaded," answered the farmer. The son had told them what terrible things had happened there, but the farmer said it was too horrible to repeat. "My son gave us this advice," he continued, "Mother, Father, you go as fast and as far as you can; just don't stay with them, (Russians)." Their plan was to go to Ventspils and on to Germany.

Arvids and Mother crossed the river and walked to the Salts' farm where they where greeted by his friend's Mother. Again, Mrs. Salts and also the other guests staying at her house warmly received them. She said her son had already left for Sweden. But a young couple staying at the farm had just returned from Liepaya, and could explain everything about the boats leaving for Germany.

The young couple told Mother and Arvids, "Don't believe all the stories about the boats sinking. Boats leave everyday and many have already reached Germany. We are also going very soon." Her husband, an engineer, had some clout and was very kind to them. He offered his horse and wagon to get our belongings and take us to the train station so we could get to Liepaya. Then he gave Arvids tickets to get on the boat!

The wondering and wandering was over. It seemed that a decision had been made. We would go to Germany! Arvids was forced to give up the idea of waiting for any news of his mother.

*Used by permission of the American Latvian Youth Association from
Rigas Rokas Gramata, 1989

5

The Escape

In her heart, Mother knew that God's hand led us through it all. Without faith, Arvids and Mother would not have known what to do or where to go. We were living with uncertain life and death circumstances, relying on God's will and quietly praying. We were escaping, and without realizing it, we had become refugees. Mother was very concerned about my health, fearing that I would not make it. I was so very frail from my bout with diphtheria and had recently had surgery to remove a cist from behind my left ear. Mother and Arvids were married by a Latvian minister on September 3, 1944 in the Lundze parish. No documents were drawn up because there was no law in the land. The legal marriage documents were issued about four years later when we were in Mannheim.

After bringing our belongings to the Salta farm, we spent the night there sleeping on big straw bags. Mother lit candles and a lantern for some light. Blankets were spread on the straw bags, but Mother could not sleep. In the candlelight, not too far from our lowly berth, Mother could see Mrs. Salta on her knees praying; asking for God's help! Mother would not forget this scene. It seemed to be etched forever in her mind. Earlier that evening, Mrs. Salta had offered all of us dried lamb's meat. Mother said it tasted good, but I don't remember. I can only recall that the straw bag was quite uncomfortable and made noise every time anyone moved even the slightest bit.

The next morning, Mrs. Salta got the horse and wagon ready and drove us to the train station. These were her parting words to Mother, "Laima, you do not have a mother to see you off, so I will be your mother." What a dear, sweet lady! She remained in Latvia for the rest of her days, living through the worst years of the brutal Communist rule.

We were traveling again. We were on our way to Germany. We would soon see Millie and Tuta again. There was a certain amount of hope, a destination, a destiny. The important thing was that we were together. We had the essential things, mainly food: the jars of jam, the dried bread slices and some smoked flounder that Arvids had bought in Ventspils. The smoked flounder tasted marvelous to me—even the dried bread pieces tasted wonderful! One time the dried fish got rained on and the flavor soaked through the dried bread pieces. We ate it anyway and enjoyed the flavoring of the fish on the bread. Along the way, we stopped at a farm with an apple orchard. The farmer sold the apples very cheaply because they too were getting ready to leave Latvia. Arvids bought several bags thinking that if we had nothing else, we could just eat apples.

Liepaya, one of two port cities, sits south of Ventspils quite a distance. As we traveled further south along the Baltic Coast, we began to hear the cannons or was it bombs again? This was not a good sign. At that moment, it had been our goal to reach the train station called Edole, and that we had accomplished. Liepaya was still further south. What to do?

"Here we are trying to get farther away from the front line, and now we are going to drive right into the Russians!" remarked Arvids.

A couple of weeks earlier, Arvids had obtained an old rickety bicycle, and pedaled to Edole to meet some people from Bauska to talk things over. He not only found out what had happened in Bauska, but to his surprise, his buddy, Rudy was there also. By the time Arvids reached the railroad station, the old bicycle fell apart. Rudy loaned his bicycle so Arvids could get back to the Piltene farm where we were staying at the time.

We got to the Edole Train Station to find it locked up tight, but Arvids found out that the train would be running to Liepaya in the morning. Again, God provided for us. One of the railroad cars was being used as a waiting room. We took our shelter there for the night as did many other people. Several German soldiers got in the railroad car and were also waiting for the train to Liepaya. Again we feasted on dry bread pieces and smoked flounder. After that Arvids went to where Rudy was staying and returned the bicycle. Rudy came back with Arvids and spent the night on the railroad car with us.

When it got dark, the soldiers lit candles. They played cards and drank liquor late into the night. We were all very tired and fell asleep easily. Mother awoke at the crack of dawn. She looked out the window and saw a soldier sprinting back toward the railroad car. He had a briefcase under his arm and Mother thought it looked just like Arvids' briefcase. When he hopped on the train car, he apologized profusely that he had mistaken the briefcase to be his own. And right there close by was an identical briefcase. The soldier said he could not loose the important "stuff" that was in his briefcase—his civilian clothes! Our baggage was elsewhere on the train, but Arvids kept the briefcase with him all the time. It was clear that the soldier had not looked inside Arvids' briefcase. All of our money was in it!

In the morning, we climbed on the train at Edole, bound for Liepaya. Rudy could not leave yet, because some of his documents were not in order. Arvids gave him the address of yet another friend from his college days now living in Liepaya, where we might be staying at a nursery and greenhouses. We arrived at the address of Arvids' friend and he promptly offered us a room at his house. The friend advised us that on the other side of the garden and greenhouses, was an air raid shelter. We should use it if needed. Arvids's friends' family was going to stay at their country home for a few days.

At the house in the city of Liepaya also stayed an older woman who looked after the place while the owners were gone. Mother was making canvas like linen covers for our suitcases and boxes so they wouldn't fall apart. She was writing the Heidelberg address on them. It was the address Millie's Mother had sent through Mirza, to us when Mother wrote to her in Tukums. Simply the address was Dr. Zilling, Heidelberg, Germany. As far as we knew, Millie would be there.

For the first two nights everything was quiet except for the bombings we could hear in the far distance. But on the third and fourth nights came the dreaded bombings over Liepaya. The air raid sirens went off and the sky lit up like a Christmas tree. It was like a million flares were falling out of the night sky in a chilling reddish color. After dark, no one was allowed to have lights on, so as to protect the city from being located by the approaching bombers. The shades were drawn all the way down.

We were all in one room together. Maris and I were put to bed at dusk. We did not sleep, however, when full darkness set in, Mother went to look in on the older woman to see if she was alright. The woman lived in a room on the street side of the house. Mother did not find her. About that time, she heard loud noises and guessed the bombs were already falling. Arvids wanted to be sure that Mother was alright and went to look for her. Maris followed him through the darkness. Meanwhile Mother was quickly trying to make her way back to our room in the complete dark. That left me in the crib, all alone, gripped with terror at the lighted sky and falling bombs. I started wailing as loud as I could, because once more I thought I might never see my Mother again. The red night sky was just too scary to be alone when you are four.

The big noises were getting louder and closer. The earth quaked, without stopping, and we could hear something falling on the roof. There was no way we could even think about running to the air raid shelter now. We had to remain in the house, come what may, while the sky tore loose with destruction. Mother prayed for our safety and survival. It seemed like the bombing went on forever, but it was probably less than an hour. The next morning, when we went out to the garden, we saw a big hole on the other side where a bomb had fallen. The greenhouse glass was shattered, and all that remained was a wooden skeleton frames for each.

Once the bombing stopped, the fire sirens started and sounded for a long time. Of course there were fires all over the city. The next night, almost the same thing happened as the night before. Arvids and Mother decided that we could not stay here for another night. We had to move on. By now the trains had all been shut down! Lithuania had already fallen to the Russian forces so it wouldn't be long before the Russians would take Latvia too.

Liepaya was full of refugees, all trying to get out of Latvia. Our boat tickets had expired so now we had to go get new ones. I can see now that it was all part of God's plan for us. Mother and Arvids were busy packing up again. The address for our Heidelberg destination had already been put on our belongings, and we would soon leave.

While they were busy packing, Rudy came to the house. He had made it from Edole to Liepaya on his bicycle. While on the road, he had been shot at from a small Russian aircraft. He simply dove into a ditch, bike and all, and waited to see if the craft would return. It didn't so Rudy pedaled on. Since Arvids had given him the address where we might be in Liepaya, he knew where to look for us. Rudy didn't think we would still be there. As he was coming toward the house, he spotted my brother and me playing outside and was thrilled that we were still there. What a happy reunion for the two friends! It also meant that there was another adult to help think matters through. Rudy was a handsome, single young man not even twenty yet. He had no family. Rudy would be traveling with us and become like a family member. Most people thought Rudy was Arvids' brother.

The Germans' last strongholds in Latvia were the two seaports, especially Liepaya. Their orders were to get all refugees out and take them to Germany to be used in German work camps for labor.

It was certain, we had no choice now but to get on a ship to Germany. Arvids got tickets for all of us for a smaller boat than most refugees were boarding. Arvids and Rudy had decided that it was safer to travel on a smaller boat. If there was an air raid, the larger ships would be the first targets. Now all we needed was to find transportation to the port.

We could get a horse and buggy in Liepaya, but nobody would take German money, as it would soon be of no value. People, however, would barter for liquor or cigarettes. Those things we had packed in suitcases back in Bauska. Soon we had transportation to get to the port.

On October 24, 1944, very early in the morning, the horse and buggy made its way to the Liepaya port with our belongings and the five of us on top. The lines to board were already long. We had to wait until noon before the gates were opened. Refugees were coming with horses and buggies from every direction, all waiting to get on a ship. Our chances of getting through the gates seemed to be slim. A man was directing the human and horse/buggy traffic to keep order. He was dressed in khaki and wearing a brown fedora. When we got closer, Arvids and Mother recognized him. He was from near Bauska, Mr. Pakulis. In Bauska he had been the secretary for Rundale Castle. Another Godsend for us! When he saw us, he let our line go through a little more often than the other lines. We finally got close enough to have our baggage loaded on the ship, but still had to wait in line to board the ship.

While waiting to board, we noticed a family in front of us with three small children. The father had hung many necessary items all around his belt; a cup, a knife, a fork, and a spoon. Right in the middle of his derriere hung an enamel bed pot. The potty swayed back and forth. It was a very comical sight, but was hard to laugh at that time. I thought the man looked a little bit crazy. My job in this ordeal was to be the official handler of our very own white porcelain bed pot. It was heavy. I felt so embarrassed! "I probably looked as crazy as the man in front of me," I thought. No matter how much I whined or complained about my embarrassing burden, I still had to carry the pot. Mother said I would be using it as much as anybody else and to stop complaining.

While still waiting to board the ship, we watched sailors carry infants wrapped in blankets onto the ship. They emptied the orphanage of about 75 to 100 babies. What a sight that was! Someone standing behind us remarked that this must be a lucky ship with so many babies were aboard. I would find out later that even though a lucky sign, the babies created an awful smell from their diapers being full. There was always the incessant crying of babies. We would never find out what happened to them in Germany.

Finally, we boarded the ship named *Lapland*. By this time the little sea vessel was almost full. Our room was at the very bottom of the ship. The room where we would sleep was intended to be a berth for many soldiers or sailors. All the spaces were taken by other refugees except for one bed made of a wooden frame with a straw mattress on it. That bed was for the five of us; Rudy, Arvids, Mother, Maris and me. The three adults were thankful that there was even a bed.

It could have been the floor for all of us. The five of us slept like sardines cross-ways on the bed.

It was October 24, 1944 when the *Lapland,* with its hatches latched, sailed out of the harbor after dark and without any lights so as not to be an easy target for air raids. That's when the bombing began. Even before the ship left, we could hear the air raid sirens blaring and the bombs dropping. Liepaya was the German's last stronghold and the Soviets did not get them out until May of 1945. For the Soviets, the Baltic seaports were crucial for shipping as Russia has no sea-coast that is navigable. The Soviets had already taken Riga by about the twentieth of October. Mother and Arvids were never to see Latvia again.

As a young girl, my Mother often wondered how sad it would be if she ever had to leave her country. She would soon find out. But now her only feeling was of great fear. She held a constant prayer vigil inside of her heart.

"Dear God, please let us survive."

6

Refugees in Germany

The *Lapland* sailed west through the night on the Baltic Sea. By morning it docked at the Swinemunde Port in Germany. My brother and I explored the little wooden ship in the morning hours before we disembarked. The stench from the infant quarters had permeated most of the area around it. It made me want to throw up. There were still a lot of babies crying. We ran past that area as fast as we could. In a corner of a small hallway was a big pile of what appeared to be salt.

"I wonder what that is?" I asked my brother.

"I think it's salt. I'll taste it, then we'll know for sure," he replied. "Ja, it's salt."

"Why do they have a big pile of salt here on the floor? Do they think people will use it here on this dirty floor?" I inquired of his wisdom.

"I think people need it in their diet. They can come and get it anytime they want," he explained.

The explanation was quite remarkable, and I thought no more about it. My brother was brilliant! That's all there was to it, he knew everything.

I don't remember much about getting off the ship, but my mother and Arvids were quite relieved that we had made it to Germany without harm. If there were planes overhead, I did not know about it.

After disembarking and collecting our belongings, we were put on a train bound for Erfurte. Now that we were in Germany, the deutschmarks Arvids had in his briefcase became a valuable commodity again. Where he couldn't use money, the liquor and cigarettes worked! How could he have known to take all of these things along when we were only going for a couple weeks of vacation? He and mother must have had a premonition, and were prepared for anything that could happen. Those distant cannons must have given them a forewarning that a change could take place. It was better to be prepared than to be sorry! Nobody had any idea what would or could happen next, but it was comforting to be moving farther and farther away from the sounds of war.

From the ship we went right to the train destined for Erfurte. Many, many refugees were shuffled to Erfurte. Having no place to go, Erfurte would get us closer to Heidelberg where we still hoped Millie was. The train with its wooden benches was very crowded with people standing everywhere, just glad to be on board. I had no place to sit and finally sat down on the floor. I was very tired, but there would be no sleeping. Just across the little isle from me, a mother had let her daughter, probably close to my age, sucking on a huge multicolored lollipop, stretched out on the entire length of the bench! This was too much for me! People were standing up on the entire route and here this spoiled brat gets to take the whole seat to herself! Maybe she was from some kind of supremacy family and had more privileges then we did as refugees? I will never know.

In Erfurte, we were taken to a German barracks for a place to rest our weary bodies. Crude as the barracks were, they were a comfort of sorts. The beds were nothing more than two-by-fours nailed together for bunk beds, without even the consolation of the straw mattresses. Then again, this was only a temporary set up until we could get to Heidelberg. I am not sure that Arvids or Rudy or Mother knew that as refugees we were all to become the workforce in Germany. The reason for the rescue from Latvia was not an act of good will! It was merely a relocation to work camps.

Erfurte, as I remember it, was a living hell for refugees. The buildings were arranged in a rectangular shape (about 6 of them) and fenced in all around the outside. These wooden structures had a building for showers, and washing clothes (by hand of course); a mess hall with army provisions; and sleeping barracks. The latrine was in a class of it's own. The latrine was a separate one-room building. The building had a wooden floor covering one half of its width and a waist high wall perpendicular to the floor. You sat on the edge of the board, doing the balancing act! There were no seats to rest your hindquarters or a comfy seat hole. You simply perched on the edge of the board and let it go! All of the waste from your body went down deep into an open holding gullet. Toilet paper was unheard of. Both men and women used the same facility without a dividing wall. There was no place for modesty in the war. The putrid stench could make a grown person vomit! For the men, the urinary job was much easier than for the women, obviously! But for me it was especially frightening. It was a difficult task for me to get up on the wall since it was built for grown-ups, not for short four-year-olds. My biggest fear was that I would lose my balance and fall over backwards into the muck! I begged for someone to hold me while I was up there. Not always did that happen and I would have nightmares many years afterwards about falling in. Today I enjoy a luxurious toilet with a heated seat and washlet to rinse off when I am finished. There is a pushbutton setting for high or low pressure spray; front spray or rear spray; oscillating or pulsating; water temperature; deodorizer and a dryer. I've come a long way from Erfurte latrines!

All buildings had an underground shelter tunnel, dark, dreary and frightening. Entrance/exit on each end meant quicker shuffling of people into the shelters. Erfurte seemed to be the hub of air raids. Anytime of the day or night we were rushed into these shelters. To a small child like me, these tunnels seemed endless, merciless!

One evening the air raid sirens seemed louder and fiercer than ever. Again we rushed into the underground tunnel. As always there was a mass of people packed into the shelter. There were men, women, children, stuffed hip to hip, butt to bust and babies crying … I had lost my mother's hand. I could see none of my family anywhere. I was totally by myself! I was a midget among all the big people. Fear and panic overcame me.

Then it struck! An American plane had been shot down and hit the building next to our barracks. An enormous burst of explosion rocked the shelter. Fire could be seen on the end of the tunnel and people started to panic and rush in the other direction. People were screaming, shouting, pushing. I was in the middle of this terror stricken crowd, feeling like I was going to be trampled or stampeded to death. The smoke started to infiltrate but what were we going to do if we did get outside alive? The end of the air raid signal had not been given. Oh, what was a child alone to do? Cry! Maybe these people will hear me and not push me over and walk on me. Somehow I did get reunited with my mother, but just how has faded from memory.

Maris, the daredevil, watched the plane come down and just before it hit, he dove into the shelter. Behind him, he could see the flames shooting toward the shelter entrance. My brother had no fear! This lack of fear is probably what made him a great staff sergeant in the U.S. Air Force years later. The shower house where he had been, about five minutes earlier, was gone and so was the mess hall. The only thing left in the spot where the two building used to be was a propeller and the engine from the plane.

The next morning, after the plane explosion, all refugees were ordered to line up outside the barracks and stand together by families. Count was taken for any casualties. As the German officers looked over each family, any male member of age was called into the German army, by now known to us as the Nazis. In our family group stood Rudy, a healthy young single male in his early 20's. He stood slightly behind us with bent knees to make him appear smaller. He looked so much like Arvids that he could pass for his son. We stood there, stoic with tongues in cheeks, and waited. The officers looked us over and went on, never detecting Rudy! God's hand had passed over us again and saved Rudy from combat duty. God was with us, always.

Arvids was a remarkable human being. Realizing that we were destined for work camps, he had to do something and fast. His extreme good looks was also in his favor. He went to the administration building to see the commander of the Erfurte Camp. With a bottle of schnapps under his arm, he entered the commander's office and walked up to the secretary, a beautiful dark haired vixen named Erika. He swooned her and got our passes stamped, "Auslander" meaning foreigner. Not only did he get the documents stamped, but also she had arranged for a truck to pick us up immediately to take us to the train station. I can still remember Arvids running across the drill field from the commander's building to our barracks waving a piece of paper over his head and shouting, "Pack up, pack up, quick! We are leaving for Heidelberg."

No sooner had he run back to us, than the truck was there. Mother and Rudy threw everything we had that was not packed away into a couple of blankets, tied them up hobo style and on the truck we went.

When we got to the Frankfurt Train Station, the train was stopped indefinitely. There was no passage across the river, Meine. The Allies' bombs had destroyed the bridge. We began to see the devastation of the bombing that had taken place before our arrival. It looked to me like half of the station had been destroyed. On one side, the wall was so damaged that it left the station open to the elements. We settled down for the night at a round table and located three chairs in the part where the roof and walls were still intact. Other people had done the same thing, and the station filled up with what were probably refugees like us. Somewhere along the way, we had acquired some warmer clothing. I know I had a coat and Maris had a navy P-coat. I don't know if Mother had made them, since we still had Charlotte's sewing machine, or if she got the clothes from someone else. After all it was now October and no longer summer weather.

Our sleeping arrangements were rather meager that night. The table and chairs became the sleeping quarters for the five of us. Since Maris was such a trooper, he slept under the table. My bed was on top of the table. The three adults sat in the chairs and rested their heads in their arms on the table. None of us had a pillow or even a blanket. It was a very difficult and cold night. We ate the old dried bread pieces and smoked fish. Those food items were our staples, which would sustain us many days. No worry about anybody getting fat or gaining weight! The meager diet did not help my frail condition, however, as we journeyed on. And thus we spent Frankfurt au Meine feasting on exotic dried/ smoked fish and gourmet, brick strength bread pieces.

Overnight, the Germans had fixed up a temporary railroad bridge, held up by big posts, which looked quite risky, but the train got across and we were on our way to Heidelberg, dear Heidelberg, and Millie!

Baiba at ten

Maris at twelve

7

Heidelberg

Other refugees, including Mr. Pakulis who helped us out in Liepaya, were talking about leaving Erfurte and heading for Dresden. It was supposed to be the safest place in Germany by far. Arvids discussed his plan with other refugees saying that his sister-in-law was in Heidelberg, and that we would head south. Everyone told Arvids that Heidelberg was the worst place to go because it was bombed daily. Go to Dresden instead! As it turned out, most people today know that Dresden became the dreaded city because of the destruction and bombing. The city was practically destroyed. Many people lost their lives. There will always be rumors in wars, and you just don't know the right thing to do. Arvids and Mother had to put their trust in God to lead us in the right direction.

It was now November of 1944 and Germany was still holding on as they started to recede from the assaults of the three big powers of Russia, England and United States.

All of our baggage had already been addressed for Heidelberg, we pushed on to our goal a reunion with Millie, come-what-may! A short ride took us out of the war torn Frankfurt and into Heidelberg at last. What a beautiful place! Was there a war going on? One certainly couldn't tell as nothing in sight looked destroyed or even damaged! This was a refugee paradise after what we had seen since coming to Germany. Arvids found the address where Millie was staying and we had a sweet reunion; the four of us plus Rudy with Millie and Tuta. Robert was still in the German army somewhere else.

This was the first time I had ever seen Millie. She was tall and thin. Very outspoken! An excellent cook, Millie could prepare a Latvian dish without effort. Her favorite was dishes with mushrooms or just mushrooms alone. She was an expert on mushroom gathering in the forests of Latvia and Germany. She knew just exactly which ones were poisonous and which ones were good. It's like she had a PhD in mushrooming!

When Millie was around, there was always humor and laughter. She saw the funny side of everything. I enjoyed being around Millie and grew very fond of her. She only had two bad habits. She was a chain smoker and loved vodka. In later years she became an alcoholic, but she never lost her humor. She conquered her addiction to both habits in her seventies with the help of AA. She spoke fluent German, read German magazines and worked crossword puzzles in German. What a remarkable woman!

Millie once told this joke: A man got on a crowded elevator and when the door closed he felt someone behind him pushing him forward. He told the person behind him to stop pushing. The voluptuous blonde behind him retorted, "Who's pushing, I'm just breathing!"

I walked with Millie many, many times when she was on a food hunt. But at the same time, she was on a cigarette hunt also. Since cigarettes were not sold anywhere, she resorted to picking up cigarette butts from the sidewalk and finishing them off to satisfy her addiction. When I walked with her, I was always on the lookout for cigarette butts too, to help her out, however I never became a smoker. I tried to smoke a cigarette just once as an adult, but couldn't tolerate the taste or the smell. I didn't even know how to hold a cigarette properly. And I must have looked like an idiot trying.

In Heidelberg, Arvids secured a job with a Nazi officer. He was hired as a gardener to care for greenhouses that cultivated flowers for their flower shop and vegetables for the café in the back of the flower shop. We were given rooms upstairs over the restaurant. Mother worked in the kitchen, and I was supposed to help set the tableware in the café. I did my best, but somehow it just didn't come out right. My brother worked to clean floors and carry dishes. For our meals, we always sat around a huge wooden table in the middle of the cafe kitchen. Hey, life was good, almost normal! We had food and shelter!

My appetite was very poor and most things put in front of me I could not stand to look at, let alone eat. Since there was no choice of food items, I was forced to partake of the precious provisions set before me. Everything was laden with onions and sometimes what looked like long stalks of boiled slimy celery. They might have been leeks for all I knew. One night we would have leeks and potatoes and the next night potatoes and leeks! Meat? No, there wasn't any. The meal was in the form of a soup with just a few potatoes and a bland, tasteless broth. Everybody else ate with delight, especially my brother, but then he would eat anything. I couldn't force down another spoonful. The German woman who made all of the provisions was insulted that I did not like her wonderful soup. I tried again at Mother's urging to eat the slippery vegetables with no taste. My stomach started to churn and my face broke out in sweat. I was sitting next to Mother and leaned over to whisper in her ear, "Mother, I think I am going to throw up!" She quickly excused me from the table and I ran outside where the vomit wouldn't be so disgusting to other diners. Mother made apologies for me to our exuberant hostess. At one time we were served split pea soup and Mother raved about how good it was. I could not eat it and made another scene. I told her it tasted like sand that was colored green. Yuk!

One day the German frau of the house took me on a tour of all of the rooms upstairs and showed me all the different toys and dolls that had belonged to her daughter. She would get them down from the top of a wardrobe, or a high shelf, let me see them and touch them, but she put them right back up. Much to my disappointment, she did not allow me to play with any of them. What anguish she caused me to suffer! Me, without any toys at all and I was only allowed to look at these gorgeous things. Why did she tease me like that?

All food items, including bread, were on coupon rationing. I was taken along whenever Aunt Millie or Mother went for some food item. It was a pathetic sight for anybody to see a small scrawny child standing in a line with a woman, and so it gave us more chance that we would end up bringing something home. A loaf of bread per week for all of us was a very precious commodity.

The air raids did not spare Heidelberg. I remember spending a lot of time rushing into and staying for hours in the underground shelter. It was always very dark and cold and no noise could a child make for any reason. The Nazi officer was usually in the shelter with us and spent a lot of time communicating on his radio. On the radio blasting away, time after time, these words have been engraved in my mind forever: "Konel-rado-sieben!" Something about number seven, although I did not understand just what! The air raids did not come as often as in other places we had been, but when they came, we took cover. More often then not, Mother, Maris and I would climb to the top of the hill and up the lookout tower where we could see the whole town instead of going to the shelter. Whenever we could, our refuge was in the tower rather than the shelter. Mother somehow felt safer up there. It did not seem that way to me, though.

When we got a small apartment, more like one room for the five of us, a daily task was to go up on the hillside just across the street from us, and gather twigs for some heat and for cooking a little something. Every day Maris and I and Mother would go and bring back sticks we had gathered. They never lasted very long and there was no heat by morning. Germany and Latvia were very similar in climate, so by December, the weather was very frigid.

Christmas, 1944, came when we were in our one room apartment. There was no Christmas tree or decorations. We had some heat from our little wood stove and sang some Christmas carols. Somewhere Rudy got a hold of some cookies to treat all of us. They were so delicious!

One morning, Mother and Arvids had already gone to the café-flower shop; Maris and I were left to our own devices. It was very cold in the room. We took off all of our clothes and were jumping on the bed stark naked to keep somewhat warm, when Mother walked in and caught us. We both got chewed out and she was visually very upset with us. I had to put my wool turtleneck sweater on after that episode. Oh how I hated wool sweaters! (I still do.) The wool made me itch terribly and I just felt like I couldn't move much. Why do kids do stupid things? Because kids do stupid things, even during the war, but I never did it again.

The air raid siren went off one day when we were on the wooded hillside picking up sticks. It was useless to try to get down in time to get to the shelter. A small dirt road wound around the hill where a military hospital stood. Not far from us was the gateway to the hospital but the big iron gate was closed. Mother quickly took me to the gateway, a giant stone monolith. It was made with large cut stones with a huge girder across the top. Mother told me to stand in the gateway so it would protect me from any falling shrapnel or debris. Then she left. I didn't know where Maris was or where Mother went? To start wailing was out of the question! I was alone and more frightened than ever. Cry? I did but without sound. Tremble and shake? Yes. But no sound did I make! No one would hear me anyway. As the planes roared overhead, I kept watching the sky and looking at that girder. If the gateway gets hit, the stones would all come down on my head. How would I know which way the stones would fall? Which direction would I run? That was the only thing I could think about, "Dear God, please help this blonde pig-tailed head to survive."

Then the awful crash came, it was not too far from where I was standing, or so it seemed. It did not look as if there was any fire but a cloud of dust roared up like Mt. St. Helen's. A bomb had hit the hospital! Mother and Maris had been on the outside of the gateway and we hurried down the hill quickly without much kindling. What the American planes were trying to target was a tunnel not too far from the hospital with a trainload of ammo. The tunnel was not hit. Sometime during the night, the Germans pulled the train out of the tunnel and away.

Our little apartment was on the third floor in an attic type space with a dormer window. Whenever an air raid was sounded, we had to open the window, so the glass wouldn't shatter from the vibrations of the airplanes. It did not matter if it was summer or winter, the window had to be opened up, or we probably would not have glass in it any more. Likewise, if we were leaving to go anywhere, the window was opened before we left, regardless of the weather.

Rudy got his own room next to ours and helped with the food hunting and stick gathering or whatever else he could during our stay in Heidelberg. Somehow Rudy acquired a handgun. Now everybody knew that no civilian was allowed to have a gun of any kind. The German government controlled all guns. Rudy hid it in our room in a cupboard that had doors. He had it wrapped in a folded sweater and concealed with other things around it. Somehow the Nazis got word that Rudy had a gun. They barged into his room and searched, but did not find the gun. They also roared into our room and rummaged through everything including the very cupboard where the gun was hidden. Rudy stood by watching, as the blood seemed to drain from his head. Another tense moment for all of us! But they did not find the gun! Had the gun been found, we would all have been taken prisoners. Dear God, thank you once again.

Across the street and to the right side of our window, we could see the oldest and most famous university in Europe, The University of Heidelberg. I did not understand what people did there, but Mother had told me that it was a very important place, a good place. It was old and dark then, but it was something friendly, something I didn't have to fear.

The coldest months had passed but we still kept our vigilance of gathering sticks for fire, as it is still our only way to have some hot food. Maris was by now going by himself on the hill to pick up sticks. Whenever he came back, his signal was to give a certain whistle and Mother would run downstairs and unlock the door for him. When the familiar whistle came, Mother rushed to the window and looked down to the street. There was Maris with a stick the size of a tree complete with all the branches. It sure was a lot of kindling! I do not remember how it was cut up, but for the first time Maris was scared to death that he would be arrested for climbing a tree and breaking off a dead branch.

At the age of five, I had no toys. I begged Mother for a doll. That was not possible Mother told me. The money had to be saved for food and there was not a store that sold dolls anywhere during war times! Then Mother got out Charlotte's sewing machine and made me a Teddy Bear like doll from some garment that could not be used any other way. There was not enough material to finish the teddy, but she found some little patches of flowery recyclable fabric, to make the bottom of the feet and arms from it. How I loved that doll! I played with it even before she got all the parts sewn on. I named it "Pucainis Pedainis" translating into Flowery Footsy. Sadly, I do not remember what happened to Flowery

Footsy. My fifth birthday came and went without flourish except for Flowery Footsy.

At the end of April, 1945, the American troops occupied Heidelberg. Germany had lost the war and Hitler had committed suicide. On the day of the occupation, Arvids was still on the German side of the front working in the greenhouses. He had his ways to get where he needed to be. To this day we do not know how he got away from the Nazi greenhouses, to the American side, without documents or passes, but he did. If somebody up above was not looking out for him, he might have been put in prison or worse. What an amazing man he was!

One morning in May, American GI's came parading in the street in front of our window. Everybody was afraid and tried to hide, especially me. But Maris the fearless trooper, ran to the window and shouted, "American soldiers are coming through town!" Mother was trying to shush him, but it was too late. They arrived casually singing, chatting; while jeeps and trucks followed behind them. In June of 1945, the war was over. The Allies divided up Germany and took over the government. We were now wards of the Americans.

Across from the University was a wine cellar, called Perkeos. It did not take long for the soldiers to discover Perkeos and they soon celebrated with wine and spirits. They shot their rifles into the air, like it was the Fourth of July, glad to be alive and the victors over Nazi Germany.

In the summer months, Maris and I were sent to gather nettles, a course herb armed with stinging hairs. Nettles grew wild in Europe and were edible. Mother would make nettle soup with these herbs especially if someone gave her some grease from something that might have been a meat of some kind. We always got nettle rash from picking the herbs as there were no gloves. I tried to pick them by placing my hand inside the hem of my dress to avoid the dreadful stingers. For all the trouble, the nettle soup didn't taste even half bad. It was much better than anything we were fed at the German café.

One time when Arvids was walking on the sidewalk, a group of American GI's drove by in an army truck. One of them tossed a carton of Lucky Strikes to Arvids. He picked it up and ran after the truck to give it back to them. The GI's only laughed and sped on. Not knowing how to return the carton or where, he reluctantly took it home. Honesty was one of his virtues. The cigarettes would come in handy for something that we might need, or maybe he'd give them to Millie?

June and July in Heidelberg were beautiful. At least this city seemed to be somewhat normal. Transportation was moving regularly, but food was still rationed. Sugar and meat were practically non-existent. American GI's were everywhere. They were always friendly and smiling. They gave us candy or gum. One day Tuta decided to take a little trip in Heidelberg and took me along. I was so excited to be actually going someplace planned. We got on a trolley car that was full of people, most of them standing up and hanging on to something. Tuta stood in the front by the door. I stepped a little farther in and immediately was invited by three good looking GI's to come and sit with them. I gladly obliged. I was not used to getting this kind of attention and I was fully enjoying it. I was having such a good time that I didn't notice Tuta had already gotten off the trolley and it was moving on to the next station. Frightened, I decided to get off at the next stop.

Here I am five years old and alone in a foreign city with a language I couldn't speak or understand. I started to cry, what else? On the bench at the trolley stop sat a woman with two children who looked to be about my age, a boy and a girl. She saw my distress and tried to comfort me speaking in German. I knew the words were kind by the tone in her voice. All I could say was, "Mamma, mamma." She understood I was lost and let me cuddle up to her. For a few moments I thought she would take me home with her and I would be her child. It was the only consolation I had. But a few minutes later I saw Tuta running towards us along side of the tracks. Immediately, I said, "Mamma!" Tuta ran to us and was visibly angry and totally embarrassed to have the German frau think she was the mother of a five-year-old child at the age of 18. I told her over and over that I didn't know how to say any other word that a German woman could understand. She never forgave me. Teenagers even then seemed to be irresponsible.

Then there was the egg incident! We somehow were rationed an egg for the two of us, Maris and me. My favorite way to eat the egg was to whip it up until it was thick and put sugar with it and then eat it with a spoon. Of course, there was no sugar but Mother had honey to mix with the egg. I insisted on cracking the egg myself and aimed it for the cup. But the cup somehow moved and the egg went on the floor shell and all! My brother was very upset with me and so was Mother. I went in a corner and cried. Maris however, scooped up the egg the best he could, picked out the shell pieces and enjoyed the egg by himself whipped up with honey.

"A bean where?" Mother asked me quite annoyed. One day when I was at my mother's side walking on the sidewalks of Heidelberg, Mother stopped for a few minutes to talk to someone by a red brick building with an outside windowsill. I stood patiently waiting. Spying a kidney bean on the windowsill, I picked it up and pondered what to do with this astonishing find. What else but to see if it fits in my nose! Yes it did! And then it went way up as I took a big breath.

As we walked on I began to regret my encounter with the bean and started to complain to Mother about the bean in my nose.

"How did it get in there?" Mother asked.

"I put it in there," I replied in a shaky voice. By now I was worried that the bean would stay in my nose forever and maybe lodge in my throat and I would die.

"Why would you put a bean in your nose?" Mother inquired, "And where did you get a bean anyway?"

"I found it on the windowsill back there, and didn't know what else to do with it." Now, I think that was one of the most stupid kid tricks there ever was, and I can't help but laugh at myself whenever I think about it. Anyway, Mother had the perfect remedy for the problem, "Just blow your nose really hard." The bean came popping out with a force and my life was spared once more. I never put a bean up my nose again, ever!

After the American occupation, Millie went to look for Robert. She finally found him in a military hospital. His right leg was shot up and had to be amputated. He was then fitted with prosthesis and returned to Heidelberg with Millie as soon as he was well enough. But he was alive and that was most important. We were all very grateful for that.

Almost nine months had passed since we left Latvia. The war was over. Arvids needed a job so it was time to move on.

*Printed in 1974, School & Library Publishing Co. in Sycamore, IL (Company no longer exists.)

8

Mannheim

During the first occupation, (1940) the U.S.S.R. took little consideration for constitutions that were in place in the Baltic States and Sovietization of the countries moved rapidly. The Soviet regime organized elections to elect people's assemblies on a ballot where only one slate of candidates appeared. The assemblies soon voted to incorporate the Baltic States into the U.S.S.R. Life for the Balts was quickly restructured and all property nationalized.

Within a year in June of 1941 the Soviets began the first *mass deportations*, which included women and children. Soviet military came to the door in the middle of the night and demanded the door be opened or they would knock it down. When the door was opened the soldiers dragged the occupants, still in their nightclothes, to the waiting trucks. Then they were placed on a freight train in animal cages stacked several layers high. These cages were just long and high enough to fit one person in a horizontal position. No food, water or bodily relief was offered for the entire three-day journey to Siberia. Men women and children were separated and sometimes never saw each other again. Such human indignities are difficult to imagine. The people were sent to regions of Siberia to work as slaves in mines and in lumbering with very little food or clothing. Most of the 35,000 Latvians deported did not survive the harsh conditions or if they returned to Latvia years later they were mentally ill. When the Germans overpowered the Soviets and came into Latvia, the deportation stopped. My frail, sickly body would not have survived the harshness. Mother had told us that we were not on the first list of deportation, but our names were on the second list.

In 1944 the U.S.S.R. once again occupied Latvia, after driving the Germans out. When the war was over, the big powers—Churchill, Stalin and FDR signed the Baltic States (and other European countries) over to the Soviets at the Yalta Peace Treaty. England and the United States were given other European countries. The agreement was to release these countries back to independence after an economic recovery. That never happened. England and the U.S. kept their part of the treaty but U.S.S.R. turned bitter to the world and the Cold War was on. Sovietization of Latvia had resumed full force and the second *mass deportation* to Siberia ensued.

Arvids' plan all along was to return to Bauska as soon as the war was over. Work his greenhouses, care for his mother, grow and sell roses; and most importantly make a life with Laima, his bride. Well, the war was over and it was hard to believe that we had all survived! With the exception of Robert losing his leg, all of us were in decent health. Even my health was improving with better food. The thought of returning to Latvia was now totally abandoned.

Our status had now changed. We shifted from being refugees to Displaced Persons; (DP's). We officially became Displaced Persons when we relocated to a former army camp in Mannheim, about 10 miles (15 kilometers) north of Heidelberg. The very first thing we had to do before we could enter Camp Mannheim, was to be powdered against any "creepy crawlies" that we might be bringing with us. They put this duster instrument down the front and back of our clothing and sprayed away. Cough, cough, cough! I wondered what that white powder was. Sure didn't smell like baby powder! Maris said it was DDT, and he knew everything. End of that discussion.

Upon arrival in Mannheim, we really began to see a lot of destruction. Only parts of buildings were standing. Some buildings, which looked like homes of families, an entire outside wall was blown off. I saw the exposed upstairs rooms. Somebody had hauled enough dirt to these upstairs rooms to plant a garden. I observed this in several places. It was one of the spectacular wonders of my world. The further we went into Mannheim, the more destruction we saw. More buildings lay in ruin than were standing intact. Then the train stopped right in front of the camp that would be our next home. There was no damage to this building at all. It was completely intact. Another wonder before my eyes!

Robert, Millie, Tuta and Rudy moved with us and we all occupied the same room. We shared the apartment with another family in the beginning. They were in the smaller bedroom and all of us in the bigger bedroom. We all shared the kitchen and bathroom. It was a bit crowded at the start, but then we were used to being crowded together. Your own private space? Nah! Never!

Robert was always in a light brown suit with matching tie and a white shirt. I cannot remember him wearing anything else. He looked like he was always ready for work, even if it was just to go play cards with his buddies. He was equally as good looking as Arvids, tall and slim, but four years older. His demeanor always appeared stern to me. He didn't seem to have much time or use for children and never had any of his own. I was mostly in awe and fear of this man. If Millie and

Robert argued with each other, I did not know about it. He didn't laugh or smile much, but loved to argue. He would play cards just to have someone to argue with him.

"What would I do in case he should yell at me?" I often wondered.

Tuta, Millie's only child was born from a previous marriage. She had just finished high school when we all fled Latvia. She was all business and serious. I don't remember her laughing or joking around. She never showed much liking for me. I felt the same way about her. The auburn haired Tuta was also slim and tall; her face marked with a little turned-up nose and a few freckles.

The camp in Mannheim was built of red brick and was enclosed in a complete square shape. The only access to the inside was a huge gate, big enough to bring Army vehicles through. The connected buildings were three stories high and our apartment was on the second floor to the left from the entrance gate. In the courtyard of Camp Mannheim was a playground, with swings and teeter-totters, some trees and a paved driveway all the way around the inside. The MP's had their security headquarters just inside the gate on the right. Their jeep sat just outside the headquarters. On one occasion, Maris got in their jeep, got it started and drove it around a bit, but abandoned it when it became too difficult. He never got caught! He was then nine years old. Like I said, he was fearless!

All of the apartments had two bedrooms, the smaller bedroom had a balcony, but the other bedroom was much larger. At first, another family moved into the smaller bedroom and we shared the kitchen and bathroom. A large kitchen with a gas stove, and running cold water at a sink made life much easier and more independent. But best of all, a bathroom! A flushing toilet, a tub and a sink, wow! Such luxury we experienced for the very first time in our lives! The water was heated on the gas stove and carried to the tub for bathing. From the bedroom side, one could look out at the whole courtyard, but from the kitchen and bathroom, you looked out onto the street. No stick gathering here! And no nettle soup or slimy vegetables! Across the street from the kitchen and bathroom windows, an archaic mammoth Catholic Cathedral stood untouched by war or war machines. Whenever the Latvians held a Lutheran service in the cathedral, we attended. I was in awe of the beautiful ornamentation inside the cathedral.

Then there was the mirror incident. I was left in the apartment alone one day and climbed on top of the dresser that had a large mirror propped on it resting against the wall. Since I was so short, the angle of the mirror would not allow me to look at myself. I found some lipstick and wanted to see how beautiful I could look with my lips painted red. I was on my knees on the dresser, when the mirror started to slide toward me. Oh what to do? I pushed myself closer to the edge of the dresser so I could somehow get a hold of the mirror and push it back up. But the mirror was way too heavy for a six-year old. By now I am just about to the edge of the dresser with the mirror resting against my knees, but still leaning against the wall. I was in a very precarious situation. My knees started to hurt very badly and if I jumped down backwards, the mirror would come crashing down on the dresser and break. If the mirror broke, I would be in big trouble, probably get a smacking.

My knees were hurting so much by now that I cried out in pain. I started to scream for help and screamed louder! How much longer can I hold on like this? I cried even louder. I was hoping the people in the other bedroom would hear me, but then I didn't even know if they were home. After what seemed like a long time, the next-door neighbor peeked in the bedroom where I was. When she saw my predicament, she rushed over to help me with the mirror. A God send! Then she said she had heard me all along but thought I was being punished by my mother and decided she better not interfere. I am so glad she did. The mirror was spared and so was my back end.

When the other family left the apartment, Millie, Robert and Tuta moved in the other room and we were like a big happy family again. Rudy was still with us. The camp was almost completely all Latvians. It was like our own little Latvia on foreign soil.

Mother told me one day that I had to have an operation because I had lost my hearing completely. I chose the clothes I wanted to wear (as if I had so many to choose from) and felt very special. The next morning Mother and I sat on the bed. She hugged me while I cried some silent tears. Was I scared? You bet! At the German clinic Mother handed me over to the doctor and the nurse. They tied my hands and feet to a big chair and propped my mouth open and then yanked out my adenoids. No anesthesia. I screamed as loudly as I could with blood running down the rubber cape. When they let my Mother come in, they untied me and told her to go walk me outside in the clinic garden. I was very weak and dizzy and told Mother I wanted to sit down. We did for a few minutes, but the doctor came out and told her that I must keep walking. I thought I would not survive this ordeal. Then I fainted! As a child I fainted easily, especially if I was tired or had some recollection of the barbaric surgery.

One day, Millie came to me in the kitchen and told me not to go in the bedroom, that Mother was very ill. I was alarmed and started to cry. Millie reassured me that Mother will be fine, but not to go see her now since I might get what she has.

"When can I go in to see her?" I inquired.

"Maybe tomorrow," replied Millie.

"But where will I sleep tonight?

"We will talk about that later. If you hear your Mother cry out loud, don't worry, she's OK," assured Millie. Likewise, Maris was told to stay out of the bedroom too, but he spent most of his time outside anyway.

The next day, on August 31, 1945, Millie came to report to me that Mother wasn't sick after all, but had a baby girl, delivered by a midwife. I had lots of questions about the event but could not understand how a baby could come out of a woman's stomach or how it got in there in the first place. They named her after a princess and also after the aster, a flower that blooms in August, which was one of Arvids' favorites. After that Mother spent a lot of time in bed nursing the baby. All clothing and diapers had to be washed by hand in the sink or in a metal tub. Clothes were dried on clotheslines in the courtyard, on the balcony, or in the bathroom. I usually helped Mother do the washing because I loved getting things clean, not to mention my love for water. I am a Pisces if you didn't guess already.

Arvids went to work as part of the American reconstruction workforce to rebuild Germany. His job was a bricklayer. It was not his favorite thing to do, but he had a family to support and was glad to have work of any kind. Besides he was very good at it. Most of the time he stayed in the work camps and only came home weekends or holidays. Arvids could work with wood too. At one time he whittled a fishing pole from an old broom handle. He attached a reel and fishing line and went fishing taking Maris along. Arvids wasn't having any luck catching anything no matter what kind of bait he tried. Maris did not have a fishing pole but made one from a pliable tree branch and attached some colored yarn to his hook. He caught fish after fish and then showed Arvids his haul. Arvids was not too pleased and never took Maris fishing again.

When the baby was about 2 or 3 months old, Mother arranged to have her baptized. The two rooms in our apartment were spruced up. Every surface was covered with some kind of a lace or embroidered white cloth. I do not know where Mother got the cloths; maybe she borrowed some and bought some others. Candles and flowers filled the room. The apartment looked so beautiful! This was my kind of element! A Lutheran Pastor came to do the ceremony and afterwards we all had something that was close enough to a feast that we called it a feast. The baptism was a wonderful, beautiful day.

A Latvian school was set up in the Mannheim camp. At age seven, I started school, when all Latvian children began their formal education. I do not know where the money came from for running the school or paying the teachers. Books were scarce and we had to share with other students. School seemed very difficult for me, but for Maris, it was a breeze! I struggled to read and I remember another first grade girl helping me and being very nice to me, almost mothering me. I did not know how to react to this kind of attention; I did not feel worthy. Today I can't even remember her name.

I made friends with several girls my age. Our pastime was playing with paper dolls that we would cut out of magazines and glue on cardboard. Then we would comb through the magazines to find clothes for our paper dolls. One friend was also named Baiba and I was at her apartment everyday to play with our paper dolls. She named all her dolls Baiba; I guess the only name she knew. Every day when I left her apartment, her mother would tell me not to come back again. Every day I left, Baiba would tell me to please come back tomorrow. When I mentioned what her mother says to me every day, Baiba said not to pay any attention to her, but come anyway. She was never allowed to come to my apartment to play. I did not understand what this was all about, and I still don't to this day. Eventually, I had to stop going to Baiba's to play and again I was crushed. I wondered what it was about me that people didn't like. This same cloud followed me the rest of my life.

The highlight of my endurance in Mannheim was when I was invited to a birthday party. I anticipated this party for weeks and thought the day would never come. I had planned out what I would wear, like I had a lot of choice! I wore my so-called white dress with the red yoke. Mother braided my hair and put a big, wide, white ribbon in each braid. I felt so very special. About ten girls attended Anita's party and she received many gifts. Among her presents was a porcelain-like doll with movable hands and legs. It was probably from her parents. I admired that doll so much and later fantasized about it in my daydreams. My daydreams had birthday parties too, but never in reality.

Maris was always outside playing with other kids his age. War games and boundary games. He had made one very special friend, Sasa (Sasha). Sasha was the only child of a widow who had lost her husband in combat and had escaped from Latvia with her son and her mother. Maris and Sasha were inseparable. They were always together; they were comrades. They would leave the camp on occasion and explore Mannheim. They would chase each other and pretend to attack each other, all in fun. The Mannheim streets were not overrun with traffic, but had some cars, trolleys and trains. The busy street outside the camp had all three. Sasha and Maris were about to cross the street and enter the camp when Sasha ran out into the street right into the side of an oncoming car. He was killed instantly. Maris stood on the side of the street and watched it all.

This tragedy absorbed my whole being. I wanted to die myself. I don't know whom I felt sorrier for, Maris or Sasha's mother. My brother was blamed for Sasha's death by everybody; including our family. The loss must have been a terrible emotional burden on him without the added blame. I was depressed for weeks and found it hard to smile or laugh. The whole school walked in the funeral march, two by two. I was in the front and helped carry a big wreath. The school children walked first to the Catholic Church across the street from us and then to the cemetery. The service seemed to take forever and we stood up the whole time. I cried and cried. The death of Sasha affected me for a long, long time.

Life seemed tough for me in Mannheim. Friends were few; school was difficult. The depression of Sasha's death had overwhelmed my soul. I had no dolls or playthings. What else can a child do but to fantasize? In my fantasy, I just closed my eyes and dreamed about all the beautiful dolls I had and how I could change the many clothes they had. There were also doll cribs and carriages and dishes—anything my heart desired, I had. My fantasy world was beautiful but mainly it was an escape from reality. The worst time came when I once uttered out loud that I wished my daddy were still alive in Arvids' presence. That remark would throw me deeper into depression. Mother took me into the other room and read me the riot act. I was never to mention my father again to anybody, but especially in Arvids' presence. I did not understand then nor do I understand now why that was not allowed. I did not talk about my dad again until I was forty. The mystery of the secret was never unlocked.

When the baby was about a year old, Mother went to the store and I was left in charge of her. Now this cute little cherub was a climber. She could get to the top of anything she wanted by pushing chairs and "whatever else there was," stacking them up, then climbing to where she wanted. While I was watching her, she climbed on the windowsill, and was standing full height looking out the window and leaning on the glass. The window glass was divided into many small panes. I watched her carefully while she enjoyed herself. Suddenly, Mother burst into the room all enraged, and grabbed the baby shouting, "Why did you let her stand on the window sill like that? Don't you know any better? If the window falls out, the baby would plunge to her death! These windows are old and rickety. Or if she falls backward, she could be seriously hurt. Don't you know any better?"

"What a dummy I am?" I thought. "I didn't think the window could fall out so easily just by leaning on it. Oh, what did I know at age seven?"

Mother had made friends with a German couple who loved to take the baby for a stroller ride on the streets of Manheim. She would point to things she saw in the street and say the words in Latvian. She pointed to the top of a house or building and say, "Dummkopf!" In German that translates into "dummy" or a "dunce." Mother and Arvids were quite disturbed about their offspring using bad words. They thought maybe the couple shouldn't take her for walks any more, if they are going to teach her bad words in German! One day when Mother was with the baby on the street, she pointed again to the top of the building that had smoke coming out of the chimney and said, "Dumi kup," which translates into "smoke is coming." Years later when out of high school, my half sister journeyed to Germany and went to the address where the couple had once lived and found them alive and well but aged. The couple remembered her and my half-sister, being fluent in German, had a very meaningful reunion!

A bunch of us girls in camp decided to go swimming in the River Neckar one nice warm summer day. I snuck out with a towel and clean underwear. Since none of us owned a bathing suit, that's how we went swimming, in our underwear. Of course none of us had a bra either. Mother had told me over and over not to go to the Neckar because the water was dark and questionable. The Neckar was not the cleanest river in Germany, but getting in the water on a hot summer day was like heaven. I willingly disobeyed Mother for the swimming pleasure. We had a wonderful time and when I got home, I was in big trouble. There was a long lecture and a scolding. I did it again, when a bunch of us girls got together and were going to the Neckar. I knew it was wrong, but my desire was greater than my sense of obedience. While still waiting under our apartment window and against the wall so Mother wouldn't see me, I was getting nervous that if some of the girls didn't show up very soon, I would not get out of there, (probably some of the girls were still trying to convince their mothers to let them go). I had told the other girls that my mother said it was OK to go to the Neckar to swim. A big fat lie! But inside I was very nervous. What if Mother sees me standing here and comes to get me? I had lied to my friends and disobeyed my mother. This cannot be good! Then it happened, mother appeared from the building and without a word, marched me up the stairs to the apartment. I was really scared about my predicament, but more embarrassed than anything else. I was promised a good spanking when Arvids got home. He did not like disobedience in his household. Trust was very hard to build back up, and it took me a long time. Luckily, I did not get the spanking from Arvids.

When the whole family went to the river, it was the Rhine River, much cleaner. Part of the beach on the Rhine had a soft covering of clover. I hated being in the clover because, I almost always got stung by a bee. And every time, Mother made me play and swim at the beach totally naked. At age seven, it was just too uncomfortable. This embarrassed me so much that it made me feel very self-conscious. This lack of self-confidence I would never lose.

I loved going to school, even though it was hard for me. The class I liked best was art. In art we were taught about shading and light, how to use watercolors, and how to draw in perspective. I also liked writing and at one time I put a little booklet of stories and poems together and called it "My Publishing."

On November 18th all Latvians celebrated Independence Day. Latvians were granted sovereignty on November 18, 1918 for the first time in hundreds of years. The Letts (as they were called in European countries) donned national costumes and sang and danced numerous folk songs. There were parades and speeches and remembrances of our slain leaders. The freedom in Latvia lasted only a very short 20 years, however, Latvians did not gather to mourn and grieve, but to celebrate their nationality. The Latvians in Mannheim put on a beautiful observance. All the festivities were held in the courtyard. A large chorus group sang folk songs a cappella. I enjoyed the folk dances the most. After speakers and recitations, the festival concluded with the singing of the Latvian National Anthem, "Dievs Sveti Latviju" (God Bless Latvia). We watched it all from the window of our apartment. Mother had tears streaming down her cheeks.

At Christmas time, the school children sang some sacred Christmas songs in the courtyard, and every school child received a gift box from some American organization, of which I cannot remember. In the gift box were pencils, erasers, colored pencils, tablet paper, toothbrush and other sundry items. The best thing in the box was a Hershey's chocolate bar. But most special was Christmas Eve at home. We even had a live tree! The tree decorations consisted of cookie cutouts and little red apples. The lights on the tree were real candles. The candles were lit while all of us gathered around the tree and sang Christmas carols. Then Maris and I were asked to read some Christmas poems. After that Maris and I received our gift. It was a big shiny red apple! I gobbled mine down right away, but Maris left his on the windowsill for days. I decided that he probably didn't want his apple to leave it sit for so many days. I was tempted to grab it and eat it, and I did! Maris of course was very upset that I would dare to eat **his** apple!

"Now you've had two apples, and I don't have any!" he complained. He was always good in math.

"I was only repaying you for shoving me out the door in Bauska, I replied. I did get in big trouble for taking his apple. Temptation overtook me and I yielded. I don't think Maris ever forgave me. Today, however, we can talk and laugh about it.

Maris was always handy at fixing things. Take the old wind-up alarm clock for instance. Mother had put it aside because it didn't work any more. Maris wanted to know if he could take it apart and see the inside of the clock and maybe he could fix it. He took it all apart and clock pieces were lying all over the table. One by one he put each clock piece back in, but had one piece left over that he didn't know where to put. He wound up the old clock and "wa-la!" it worked! We figured that the extra piece is probably what kept it from working properly.

I loved to color and make the pictures look so pretty and perfect. One day I found a paper with all different kinds of hoofed animals. I colored all of their hoofs red and then started to work on the bodies. When Tuta came home and saw her animal paper with red hoofs on each of them, she started to scream and yell. This was a homework paper and was due the next morning. Boy did I get reamed out for this one! I still think I did a beautiful coloring job. Yes, stubborn I was!

In January of 1947, the winter was harsh and the frost had covered the north side of every tree and object it could cling to. It was a beautiful sight with the snow on the ground and frosted trees. On January 24, 1947, Mother delivered another baby girl and she was named for the beautiful frost outside. Three months later, Mother prepared one more wonderful baptism celebration.

When my youngest stepsister was almost a year old, it was time for our Independence Day Celebration on November 18th. Mother and Millie had prepared the food and everything was set on the table ready to eat. Mother had made meatballs, a very special treat for all of us since meat was available only about once a week or less. All of us went into the bedroom to watch the Latvian Celebration from the window, but nobody noticed that the youngest member of the family stayed in the kitchen. When all of us returned to the kitchen, to our amazement and disappointment, she had climbed on the table and finished off the entire bowl of the meatballs. Today as an adult, she does not eat much beef. But me, I crave for it like a starved wild animal robbed of its food. It must have been the depravation of the meatballs in Manheim that brought this on! Laugh, laugh, laugh! Yeah, that's what it was!

9

Schwabisch Gmund

Our two years in Mannheim were memorable. Two little girls were born, and we stayed in the best living quarters we had ever experienced. Manheim Camp was created for GI's and their families. And now it was going to become apartments for German citizens. It was time for us to move on.

Looking around Germany, Arvids and Mother could not see any opportunities or a future here in Germany. Mostly everywhere you looked, there was destruction. Going back to Latvia was out of the question, since the Communists seized all private and government properties. Arvids couldn't help but think about how his mother was doing? No mail was getting through, and if it did, it might cause harm to the recipient in Latvia.

As many other people were doing, we also applied for visas to emigrate to the United States or better known to us as America! America was perceived as a land of riches where everything was available: peace, land of milk and honey! All of us wondered what the looking box (TV) was like? For me, there would be many paper dolls and real dolls and dancing lessons. We all dreamed about this wonderful place called America!

While the paperwork was being processed, we with many other Latvians were sent temporarily in Scwasbish Gmund, another empty GI camp. The camp was on top of the hill outside of the town. Six stone buildings covered with stucco were set in a rectangular arrangement. The building on the end towards the road was a multi-purpose edifice. The second floor of this building housed the classrooms where I started second grade. School was only half a day, so everybody headed home at noon for homework and to play. Soup was served every day in the mess hall after the last class of the morning. Even **I** liked it! Children brought their own slice of heavy duty, hearty rye bread to eat with the soup.

On the first floor of this same building, was the bakery/bread store where I used to stand in line to buy a loaf of bread in the afternoon. I was with a good friend named, Aija (Aya) Baumans. She was a preacher's daughter, and was a very good friend to me. As we stood in line for the loaf of bread, a man about two persons behind me started talking to me. I knew him, but couldn't think of his name.

"I hear that you are a very good student and do excellent school work. You will be very successful someday!" said the man.

"Thank you very much," I replied sort of blushing. I never thought that I was so exceptionally good in school. But if he thought so, I wouldn't disagree with him. That one solitary comment did so much for me that I actually thought I **was** a good student and from then on I worked harder and got better grades. I never forgot those words and they helped me all the years of my school learning. I praise God for sending this man my way to give me some confidence that I so greatly lacked.

For fun, Aya and I used to go out on the street corner that passed by the camp and write down car license numbers on tablets. One day I showed mother what Aya and I had been doing, and she immediately put a stop to it. Somebody might think we are spies and arrest us. End of that entertainment! Aya's family moved to America. I never saw or heard from Aya again.

After Aya left I played with Gita Millers. Like Aya, she was an only child and her parents doted on her. Our friendship was terrific even though there were big differences in our lives. I admired her for her good life and for her beauty. Her hair was shiny brown and her skin nicely tanned. We played mostly at her house. We parted when it was time for her family to go, and I never heard from her again either.

Schoolwork started to become easier and I enjoyed it more. At the beginning of each school day, all the students gathered in one small empty room for devotions. There were Bible readings; the Lord's Prayer; and hymn singing. Except for a couple of boys, all of us were Lutheran and came to devotions willingly. One morning, I had really poured on the cheap perfume to my coat lapel. I started to feel funny and wished I could get away from my coat lapel! The room started to get fuzzy and at that moment I thought this is what it must feel like to die. After that, I remembered nothing. When I came to from the faint, I realized I was still alive but didn't want to experience fainting again.

After devotions, all students went to their first class in the morning and stayed in that room the rest of the school day. The teachers moved from room to room. Nobody ever got out of line. My best grade was always in behavior, actually the only high mark I got. The girls wore wooly long sleeved dresses, a black pinafore over the dress and long brown cotton stockings. The boys wore long pants; button up shirt and a jacket. When a student met a teacher out of the classroom scene, it was an expected custom to show respect to the teacher in a curtsey for the girls or a bow for the boys. One day a week, after school, we would come dressed in our "gym outfits" and gather in the huge courtyard for calisthenics. All students did the same exact routine at the same time. What a sight and what fun! I loved the movement because it reminded me of dancing. And I began to like school a lot! Calisthenics was often used as a performance at ceremonies.

For Christmas, the school students put on choral concerts, folk dances and other dances. The second grade girls were dressed like little angels with golden scepters in our hands and golden garlands in our hair. We danced to some beautiful music, which I thought was ballet. From that event, I fell in love with ballet. It would become my passion, my expression, my sanity and my exercise. But I would not have the opportunity to do ballet until I was forty years old. Such was destiny!

When we first arrived in Schwabish Gmund, our "apartment" was the largest room on the first floor. Three families were squeezed into this "big room" with cabinet and blanket dividers. We were used to the crowding. With us were also Rudi, Robert, Millie, Tuta and mother's newly acquired granny, Oma. She was an elderly lady all by herself, and Mother took her in as one of our family members. Oma had one daughter, also named Baiba, who she didn't have much to do with her mother. My mother had a very soft, kind heart for people. Oma became like a grandmother to us. She helped Mother and watched my little sisters. We all came to love her very much. From then on, I became Little Baiba and Oma's daughter was referred to as big Baiba. Oma's Baiba was a beautiful woman. I now would compare her to the Marilyn Monroe type. We parted with Oma when we left for "the land of milk and honey," America. A sponsor called her to San Francisco where she lived the rest of her life. We never saw her again, but Mother corresponded with her until Oma's death in the 70's.

Robert, Millie and Tuta did not stay with us very long in Gmund. Robert could not do manual labor because of his artificial leg, so they moved to another town where Robert could work in an agricultural laboratory. At one time, Robert and Millie came to Gmund for a visit. He brought something very special for us. He had a suitcase full of lobster that was already cooked. What a feast we had that day!

After the other family moved out to their own quarters, we had the whole room to ourselves. This room must have been an officer's living quarters, Arvids judged, by all the gruesome reptile-like murals on the walls. The murals were very grotesque and frightening to me. We were told it was the biggest room on the entire camp. Two large windows, cranked to the outside facing garden plots.

These plots were divvied out to anyone on camp who wanted to have a garden. Of course, we had a garden and my brother and I mainly tended it. We had cabbage, beets, lettuce, tomatoes, cucumbers, onions and dill. (Did you know you could tell a Latvian by the dill on his/her breath?) Other gardens had very tall leafy plants called corn, but for the life of me, I could not figure out what part of this plant a person could eat!

On one end of each of the concrete three story buildings were all the bathrooms, and yes, flushing toilets and cold water sinks. On the other end of the buildings were the showers. Except for the large officer's room, all three floors were set up the same way. The warm water was turned on once a week on a certain day and certain time for showers. The men and the women were scheduled at different times of the same day. This is also where the women washed the clothes. If they had a metal tub or even a washbowl, the task would be accomplished. The ceiling held all the showerheads in what seemed to me a very large room. If you got your head all soaped up, (forget shampoo, it didn't exist to our knowledge, Fels-Naptha was more like it), and it was time for the water to be shut off—too bad! If you missed the time and the day of the showers, thy stinky body had to wait until "thee" next week. Then there were times when the water was only cold! But running water was still a luxury!

In the middle of the building was a kitchen of sorts. It had no inside wall, but was a big open area with black, cast iron gas stoves lined along the three walls in a u-shape. The women would bring their food to this area to cook and then carry it back to their rooms. Maybe one or two stoves had an oven. The dishwashing room was adjacent to the stove area with sinks and of course, cold running water. Again, the women would heat the water on the gas stove and carry it to their apartment rooms to wash the dishes, or they used the sink area. Paper plates, you ask? Paper plates did not exist.

Once in a great while, when she had the ingredients, Mother would make a cake. This happened maybe two to three times a year, but I don't remember what the occasions were. It was such a treat for us! I remember sitting at the table and looking at it, waiting for my piece. Maris said it was as good as rye bread. In those days there was no margarine and butter was a rare commodity. What we put on our rye bread was lard! Yes, lard and it tasted very good too! Most of the goods we bought were from a basement store in one of the other buildings across the courtyard from us. It was probably a former PX for the GI's. Oh, yes, there were no plastic or paper bags either. We brought a basket or a small blanket to carry the purchased items home, not that there were so many items that we had trouble carrying them home.

Mother used to make a concoction that was supposed to be healthy for children. She called it "sudarbiksis" or something like that. Some of the ingredients I can recall were: yeast, sugar, sliced apples, rye bread pieces, vinegar, and beaten eggs poured into an enamel pan. Then she put it on the windowsill until the mixture fermented, which was probably about a week. As disgusting as it may sound, it really tasted like a delicatessen dessert. I have not been able to find any such recipe in any Latvian cookbook. I wish I had asked my mother what all she put in it, but now it is too late. Then there was always the dreaded cod liver oil by the spoonful every day. Yuk! Yuk!

When we did have milk, there was no refrigerator to keep it in, so it usually turned sour by the next day. That was when Mother made buttermilk, and what little butter could be eked out of the soured milk. Most of the time, Maris and I drank coffee, because that is all there was except water from the sinks.

Whatever furniture we had, was left in the room by the homebound American GI's. Just inside the door to the right were two crude open shelf cupboards where all of our kitchen stuff was kept. A large wooden table sat in the same area with a few chairs. The rest of the room was divided into bedroom sections separated with metal wardrobe cabinets.

On the opposite end from the cafeteria/school, was a concert hall, with a large stage. The building was big enough to hold several hundred people. Mother took me there often for concerts, plays and ballets. It was definitely the entertainment area for the GI's. I took in every performance I saw with great awe and was enthralled with each. This is what I wanted to do when I grew up. Perform on stage. In this theater is where I built my future dreams. Then, if I ever had children, I would have twin girls and dress them alike. No boys. Ah yes, these were but pipe dreams of a young girl living as a refugee.

When Arvids came home from his work leave, we usually had a nice meal and at times take walks together. On occasion, we even took some pictures. On one such time we planned to climb the hill we could see from our camp, Mt. Rhishbergs. We all got dressed up and walked into town, then up the other mountain following a trail. It seemed awfully far to me, but I trudged along with the rest of them. My little sisters had to be carried most of the way. On the way back up to our camp, we were all pretty well tired out. A bus full of soccer players stopped and offered to take us up to our camp. Arvids gratefully accepted and we enjoyed listening to the players harmonize some lively German tunes a cappella. These were the memorable moments, not easily forgotten.

I still had an immense fondness for rabbits. Somehow I was able to get two rabbits. One rabbit was black and white and the other was all white. One of them might have been my brother's rabbit, however. The cages for rabbits were already available, just behind the camp buildings. So I was given a cage for my rabbits and I took care of them every day. I brought them peelings, old bread pieces, grass and clover. Just about every day Maris and I would take our little sisters and go in a nearby clover field to pick some fresh clover for the rabbits. What we didn't know is that the field belonged to a German farmer. He didn't like our clover picking in his field. One day unbeknownst to us, the farmer was hiding in the bushes. Just as we started to pick the clover, he came running at us with a pitchfork and yelling something in German. Maris grabbed our youngest sibling and I dragged the other one by hand behind me as we took off for our lives. Maris would not abandon the pail of freshly picked clover. This was actually scarier than the war, I thought. We never went in that clover field again. Sorry bunnies!

One day I noticed the black and white rabbit making a nest. What excitement that was for me! Then the day came when the baby rabbits arrived. I couldn't believe my luck to have baby rabbits! A group of us kids gathered at the cage every day to watch the bunnies grow and sleep.

I remember this time so well because it was when I, at age eight, first found out about the birds and bees!

One of the girls in the group standing around the rabbit cage decided to post a question to me, "Do you know how babies are made?"

"Yes, they grow in the mother's stomach," I answered kind of sheepishly while the other kids all giggled.

"No, you dummy, the man and the woman put their hind ends together and it makes a baby."

"How disgusting!" I thought. "I'm never going to do that! Yuk!" I did not say another word, I couldn't. I was too embarrassed. But it was certainly significant news in my life!

We could also have a small chicken coup enclosed by a high chain link fence. The pen had a roof and was very sturdy. The GI's must really have liked animal keeping to go to this much trouble! It was Maris' and my job to take care of the animals. We had about nine pullets and a rooster, I think. Even though we had no mash for the chickens, they laid some eggs anyway. Eggs were such a rare treat for us.

In chicken society, there is always one chicken that the rest of them will pick on. Mother named the outcast pullet, Ieppy, because that is what she sounded like; iep, iep! We were to handle her with care and make sure she got something to eat every time we brought them oats. Every day I would go to the chicken coop and hold Ieppy and pet her. We all felt sorry her. One morning Maris and I found her dead in the coop. I was so sad again. Then I began noticing that every-so-often a chicken would disappear. When I asked Mother about this, she made some excuse and I asked no further questions. The chickens kept disappearing until there were none!

At Gmund we always had things to do. Maris was in the Boy Scouts and I joined the Girl Scouts. Our uniforms were made of used American Army khaki uniforms. I felt much honored to be part of this group. It was a shot in the arm for my self-confidence. We met once a week and were classified as junior Girl Scouts. The senior Girl Scouts were our leaders. We were divided into groups of six or seven in each. Each group had a captain and a co-captain. The girls who earned the most merit badges got to be the captains first. And it was usually the older girls who accomplished this. Some of our activities included, all kinds of games, going on hikes and singing songs.

Once a year we went on a camping trip. I loved our camping trips. The Boy Scouts went too! We had to get up very early in the morning and dress in our scouting uniforms. We carried any items we needed and marched in a line, two by two to the campsite. The boy scouts pitched their tents to stay the five days but the Girl Scouts were not allowed to stay overnight. In the morning, we played games and after lunch all of us were sent out to pick wild strawberries for our dessert for supper. All the strawberries were dumped together and divided for everyone. Mothers of the Scout troops' provided the rest of the food. After the berry picking, we all had to take a nap. Then we played more games and always sang songs.

Once a year, the Scouts held a jamboree in the evening. We all sat around a big bonfire singing songs and playing different games. Each Girl Scout had to make a wildflower garland before the ceremony to wear with the uniform.

The Scouts always took part in any kind of a national ceremony or celebration of any kind. I loved (and still do) ceremonies and performances, especially if I was part of it. Finally, I belonged to something.

There came the time when I was to earn my cooking badge. I left the scout meeting and went to our so called apartment, peeled several potatoes, sliced them, and fried them up in skillet with lard. I rushed back over to the meeting with my food treasure and the troop gobbled them up like they were cookies. The scout leader said it took too long but they were very tasty. And so I earned my badge.

A day was planned when an American plane would fly over the camp and drop bags of candy for all the children. The Scouts were all dressed in their uniforms and were lined up around the courtyard on all four sides. Everyone in the camp came outside to watch this wonderment. The Latvian and American flags were displayed and a big white X marked the center of the courtyard to give the pilots a clear target. I don't know how long we stood there waiting for the plane, but it seemed a long time for me, yet no one moved, complained or whined. Finally, we could hear the plane at a distance. The excitement rose within me as I watched the plane come overhead and move right on by us. What a disappointment! Then suddenly, we all spotted something dropping out of the airplane, but they had completely missed the mark and the candy bags fell somewhere else. Maybe the wind was blowing in the wrong direction that day? Who knows? Some people started running down the hill to where they thought the candy must have hit the ground, but I never did get any. Such was the life of a refugee girl, its excitements and its disappointments.

For the longest time, I begged Mother for a white dress. So, one day when she got some used clothing, she had a lady make a white dress to surprise me. Only it wasn't the white I had hoped for, but a more beige-like color with darker flecks through it. The yoke in the front and the back was red. Very well made and a nice dress, but I showed my disappointment and it saddened my mother.

With the exception of doing his daily chores, Maris was off doing things with his friends. Climbing trees was one of their favorite pastimes. There were about four boys who decided to climb the tree that day. It was a great pastime except that all four decided to climb on the same branch, kind of a dead one. The limb broke and four boys hit the ground like falling apples. Maris injured his side on a small pointy stump but never told anyone, especially mother, for fear of getting in trouble. He took care of the wound as he had been taught in scouting and went on with daily life.

The last days at Gmund were coming to an end. Our paperwork had been completed and we were called to a small village in Pennsylvania. The Lutheran Church was our sponsor. It was sad but also exciting! Many of my friends' families had already left. On the last day, a friend of my mother's had invited us for dinner and had prepared a wonderful meal.

As we sat around the big table I inquired, "What kind of meat is this?"

"It's chicken," I was told.

"Then why does it have four legs?"

"There is more than one chicken here, that's why," came the reply.

Not for one minute did I believe it was chicken. I **knew** what it was! I could not eat any meat that day!

Maris and Baiba in Schwabisch Gmund

10

On the General Taylor

Our time of waiting was a span of two years, and now it is drawing to a close. Schwabisch Gmund started to appear like a ghost town, since so many families had already left for different parts of the world. Some went to Australia, Argentina, England, France and many like us were called to America.

Leaving Gmund was like a chapter closing in our lives as a brand new world was opening and waiting for us. It was a sad occasion, but exciting at the same time. What did this new land have in store for us? Would we have all those things we never had in our past? I was already fantasizing about clothes and dolls and doll clothes.

I had gone into town with mother a couple of weeks before our scheduled date to leave. As we walked back up the hill mother paused by the side of the road, put her arm around me, to admire the lovely field of wild flowers. There were colors of yellow, white, blue, orange and red. A breathtaking sight indeed!

"This may be the last time that we see such a beautiful sight here in Germany," announced mother. How right she was! These are the moments I hold close to my heart, because they gave me a sense of awe for nature and to appreciate its beauty. And most important, there was a bond between mother and me.

For months, Arvids had been making wooden boxes of tongue and grooved boards. He made six of them, about 3 x 3 x 4. Each box had handles on the ends. When Arvids made something, it was meant to last, and so strong you could park an army tank on it. These six boxes were to hold all of the belongings we could bring along. Charlotte's Singer sewing machine was one of the items included in a box. He varnished them and had mother paint our name and address on each box with stencils and black paint. It said:

A. KALNINS
LIBERTY, PA

The problem was to find out where in Pennsylvania this Liberty was. Zip code was not invented yet, but would be years later, right here in our own Williamsport. Arvids acquired a map. There was a Liberty in New York state very close to the New Jersey and Pennsylvania border. Arvids didn't think that could be the one, because it is really in New York. Another Liberty was on the map near Pittsburgh. Could this be the one? Then still another Liberty was in the northern mountains of Pennsylvania. Maybe this is it? When a contact was made with The Lutheran World Federation (LWF), the location was clarified as the one near Williamsport, PA.

Arvids and mother had received two other sponsors before the Liberty one and both of them also by the LWF. One was in South Carolina where Arvids would work as a logger cutting down trees for lumber. This one did not appeal to them so they rejected it. Arvids does not cut down living plants; he likes to make them grow instead. The other calling was in Connecticut. Arvids was to go work as a bricklayer. Being a horticulturist by trade, laying bricks all day in the hot sun didn't attract him either. When the third call came from a Lutheran Parish in Liberty, PA, they decided that we better take this one, since we may not get another call. Arvids would work at a saw mill for a two year indenture with pay. The church would pay rent on a furnished little house, also for two years. Arvids liked this location since it was in the country and perhaps he could restart his greenhouse business.

Our three-month journey to America was about to begin. The first camp for the immigration process was located in Ludwigsburg. The temporary shelter was old army barracks. The duration of the stay was usually a few weeks, and when that phase of processing was done, we moved on to the next camp. Rudy was no longer with us because he had already made his way to America in New Jersey. He tried to send us money by mail but we only got it about once or twice. After that it was stolen every time. Arvids had to tell Rudy not to send it anymore.

Being in Ludwigsburg and not visiting King Ludwig's palace would have been like being in New York City and not seeing the Statue of Liberty! The opulent palace, built during the rule of Duke Eberhard Ludwig between 1704 and 1733, is one of the most beautiful baroque palaces still used today for receptions and theater. It boasts 452 rooms spread over 28 buildings. We cannot be this close to a palace and not go see it!

The four of us with the two toddlers in tow, arrived at the palace on foot. I was so excited that I was beside myself. I couldn't wait to see the king and the queen! I had never seen any place so gorgeous! And then we entered the hall of mirrors. Everything was made of mirrors: the ceiling, the walls, the furniture, except for the floor, I guess because ladies who wore dresses (and they all did) could not walk on the floor for exposing their underwear. I thought this was a very appropriate decision including a lady like me. Ha, ha! Being in that palace made me feel like I was a princess with a beautiful princess dress and tiara! What a dreamer I was!

Finally, we were entering the throne room. With excitement and trepidation, my eyes glanced around the enormous room and rested on the thrones of the king and queen—but the thrones were empty!

"Where are the king and queen?" I asked mother.

"They don't sit here all the time," she said.

"Are they in another room?"

"They probably died a long time ago," mother tried to explain further.

"Oh, no! Why did they have to die before I could see them?" I was almost in tears as the princess thoughts drained from my mind while I stared at the empty thrones.

After that it was back to our humble barracks and a meal of soup for the evening. It was October now and the weather was getting cold. Keeping warm was the order of the day. The darkness came early and we went to bed as the chickens did, very early.

From Ludwigsburg, we were shuffled to the next immigration processing camp in Rotenburg. Rotenburg Camp was very close to the communist border of East Germany. The only device that separated the east and west borders was a barbed wire fence. It meant nothing to me although I was ten years old.

Old wooden barracks provided us with shelter. As long as we could go out and pick up sticks, we had a little heat from a small wood-burning stove. Maris was given an axe and his job was chopping stumps for firewood. It is now November and the ground is covered with a heavy blanket of snow. Our duration in Rotenburg was close to a month. Since I had nothing to do and no playthings, when I got tired of amusing my two little half-sisters, I would put on my entire winter garb, and go out for a walk in the woods. The woods were so quiet, white and appealing. I was a kind of a loner anyway, so these solitude walks nourished my isolated soul. Each day I ventured for my little walk. One day I decided to bring some breadcrumbs with me. (Like that was allowed with our own dire need for food.) But sometimes I did things like that just because I wanted to do them.

I followed all kinds of animal tracks in the snow, but mostly rabbits. I left some breadcrumbs by each track hoping the rabbits would come tomorrow and find the crumbs. I followed many different kinds of animal tracks, which drew me further into the woods. I would only guess what kind of animal it was by the size and shape of the paw print. I had no books or pictures to compare them and so I just enjoyed what I saw. Never once did I see the footprint of a human shoe. Suddenly I realized that I had come up on a barbed wire fence and could not go any farther. Though it looked foreboding, I was not afraid but simply followed my own tracks back to the barracks. I had not realized how fast time had slipped by and I arrived back at the barracks at dusk, a little hungry but more fearful of my irate mother for disappearing all afternoon when nobody knew where I was! I got a good admonishment that day.

"Do you have any idea how close you were to the Communist border?" Mother demanded.

"No!"

"You could have been kidnapped or shot for trespassing so close. They might even think you are a child spy!" mother continued to impress the danger of it all for me.

"I didn't mean to do anything wrong, I was just looking at animal tracks in the snow," I reasoned.

"Don't you ever do that again! Is that clear?"

"Yes."

The next day I went out to the woods again because I wanted to see if any of the breadcrumbs were taken. Of what I saw most of them were still there. I did not go very deep or stay too long since I knew I was just asking for more trouble. Nevertheless, I was not sorry for following the animal tracks the day before since I enjoyed myself so much. It was the only fun time I had had in a long time. And thus I pardoned myself for being selfish, mischievous and disobedient.

Our next stay in the immigration process was in Bonn, the capitol of then West Germany. Bonn was quite a distance north of Ludwigsburg and Mannheim and on the west side of Germany near the Belgium border. Now we are six people and six boxes on a train bound for Bonn. In Bonn like in the other places, again we stayed in army barracks, with outhouses and cold water bathing facilities unattached to the dormitory barracks. The immigration process continued with physicals, x-rays, shots, and the disinfecting of our bodies with a powder that was puffed in under our clothing. My little sisters were too young to understand and cried a lot. I was embarrassed and shy and hated every minute of it. But Maris took it all in stride like a trooper, just as he always did. The United Nations Relief and Rehabilitation Administration, (UNRRA) physicians must have thought we all had the cooties!

Finally, we are on the way to Bremen, just a quick stop since now our paperwork and physical exams are all finished, then on to Bremerhaven, the seaport which would take us out of Germany to a new world, America. The process had taken three long months.

Docked at the seaport was the biggest ship I had ever set my eyes on. Suddenly, I was very frightened and felt very insignificant. How would this huge thing stay on top of the water all the way across the ocean? So much gray steel and so many decks! I knew that soon I would be walking up the wide ramp to get on this mammoth monster and it was very scary! There was no way out of this one. It was either get on willingly or be dragged on kicking and screaming. Oh, I wouldn't dare make a scene now! Putting one foot ahead of the other, I slowly made my way up into the ship and felt like the ship had swallowed me. I was like an ant crawling on a John Deere 4850, a giant among tractors.

The ship was christened General Taylor. It carried army troops in war time. Now it was full of us immigrants, men, women, families and children. Our beds hung on hammock like canvas cloths in three tiers. The purpose of the hammock was to keep the person from rolling out when the ship tipped back and forth. The bottom birth was just plain pine boards and it is where I slept with mother and the little girls. Maris and Arvids used the hammock berths in another part of the ship. General Taylor sailed away from Bremerhaven on December 17, 1950.

It was quite crowded as usual and men were in separate quarters for of close knit hammock berths. The bathrooms and showers were in a separate area but with flushing toilets and tepid water for bathing. Men and women shared the same but everything was enclosed with a door for privacy. What I always wondered about back then is where did all the dirty water go when toilets were flushed, in the sea? Maris said that, of course, it goes in the sea. He was very sharp-witted and I believed him.

The first three days, I explored the ship with Maris. It was amazing how much of this ship there really was. All doors were about twelve inches off the floor so you had to step over each one. I thought that was odd until Maris explained why it was that way. Every part of the ship could be sectioned off when the door was shut and sealed with a big steel lever. The water would not leak from one area to the other. This was a safety device in case the ship began to take on water in one area. Somehow, I did not think it would work. For the sake of fear, I doubted everything!

On the main deck was a big swing set and a slide, obviously put there for children to play on. I just figured that children must have traveled on this ship before to give reason for a swing set. It was probably children of American soldiers, but Maris explained that the swings were put there for the children of DP families and that this ship had made other journeys like this one. This made a lot of sense to me and I marveled at my brother's capability to reason things out. What didn't make sense to me is why a swing set was needed on a ship that already rocks and rolls and swings. Did a child need to get even more motion challenged?

At the very bottom deck was the library/game room. I never saw so many books in my life but they were all in English. I could not read them except in pretend, so I just looked at them because I liked books. We played cards and checkers and chess—looked at magazines. Maris was an excellent chess player and I could never beat him, so I stopped playing chess because I couldn't stand to lose all the time. The most entertaining game to us and the other kids our age was the highly appropriate game of *Battleship.* We played that over and over and never got tired of it. There was no board game for *Battleship,* and the only items we needed for it were a sheet of quadrille paper and a pencil, where we could plot our ships and attack the opponents.' One-quarter inch quadrille paper was standard Latvian letter writing paper, so it was a bit more available than just plain white paper. Manipulatives were not necessary if you had paper and pencil.

The mess hall or cafeteria was a special experience. For the first time, I was eating American food and for the first time looking at a black man, his face shiny as an apple. I picked up a tray and pushed it along a ledge as everybody else did. As I went by the selections on the steam table, the workers behind the counter piled on great big gobs of food. I had never seen so much food! There was meat; beef, chicken, fish, pork, ham. Billows of mashed potatoes and gravy rolled onto my tray. Then there were beans, peas, carrots, squash, and some yellow bits called corn. Remembering the tall corn plants I had seen in Gmund, I still could not figure out where on that plant these yellow things were? The mystery would be revealed to me later that year. The food was very, very good, but how was I going to eat all of this. My stomach was close to the size of a small plum. I was always taught to clean my plate, and never throw away any food. I looked for rye bread in the food line but did not see any. There was this soft white square of what was soft like cake but not sweet at all. I asked Maris, "What is this?"

"American bread," he announced.

"This can't be bread, it is too soft, I think they forgot to put sugar in it," I pressed on. Somehow I knew Maris knew the whole story about American bread but this time I wanted to doubt him. But again, as usual, he was right. I had to accept American bread like it or not.

At the end of the serving line stood a very tall black man who was serving up the chocolate pudding. My eyes went up and up until I reached his face. He had a smile from ear to ear and he showed his pearly whites and said something to me in English. I could only smile back. It was the first time that I saw a black man up close. Next, I took my overloaded tray to the long tables that were bolted to the floor for obvious reasons and had an inch standup rim around the edge. I would soon learn why the rim was there. The other kids and I would sit down at the tables on fastened round stools to begin the chow down. But suddenly, the ship would tilt one way and all the trays would slide down the table and were stopped by the little rims put there so the trays don't slide off the end of the table. When the ship swung the other way, the trays would all come sliding back close to where they started. But you had to watch which one was your tray otherwise you would end up with somebody else's tray. These sliding trays became like a game with us to see if you could get your own tray back. After that game became old, we just hung on to the trays so they didn't slide.

For several days Maris and I had noticed a large crate of oranges in the hallway by the mess hall. We wanted one really badly and were willing to try to swipe a couple. But we could never find the right opportunity, as there was always somebody around watching. One day we noticed that no one was anywhere near the orange crate. We ran over to it and each grabbed a couple of oranges. Right at that moment, a man stepped into the hallway and caught us red handed with the oranges. We started to run, but he motioned for us to come back and take more. Though, we could not understand anything he said, we however could understand his hand gestures and his friendly smile. The oranges were put there for the passengers to eat for vitamin C content.

On the third day at sea, nobody was going to the cafeteria except Maris, because everybody was standing around garbage cans throwing up, including me. Three days of this sickness and there was nothing in your stomach but the bitter bile which was all that came up even with a drink of water. People were assigned turns to clean up after each other at which time the scrubber would start upchucking again from the foul smell. Then he/she would clean again!

With water all around us, for days and days, I wondered if we would ever see land again. The mighty ship just kept dipping from one end to the other. When the sea was rough, the water would splash over into the ship and horrified me. It always looked like the boat was going under water, then like a miracle would lift up again. It was probably a good thing that I had never heard of the Titanic.

On the seventh day aboard the General Taylor, it was Christmas Eve. In the social room a big Christmas tree was decorated and lighted with electric lights, a phenomenon I had never seen before. I had only ever seen real candles lit on a Christmas tree.

Since there would be no celebration or presents, we stayed in our respective sleeping area. Suddenly we could hear familiar Christmas carols being sung by children's voices. Then the arrival of a young girl dressed like an angel and carrying a flickering light appeared out of nowhere. She was weaving her way through the rooms where all the people were huddled. Old St. Nick followed her with a big bag slung over his shoulder. Many, many children were following this processional. So, I got in line too, and the procession continued through the entire ship until every child had joined the group singing Silent Night, whether they knew the words or not. The procession ended up in the big hall with the Christmas tree where all the adults had also gathered and were seated in very nice chairs. The Christmas Eve service began, followed by gifts for all the children. Each child received a Hershey bar, a white handkerchief and a Red Cross school kit. The kit contained pencils, colors, a tablet, erasers, a thing they called a pen (but you didn't have to dip it in the ink well), a ruler, small scissors, a pencil sharpener, tracing shapes and gum. It was the most memorable Christmas I can remember. Christmas Day was celebrated with another church service and a turkey dinner in the mess hall. By now most people had recovered from the seasickness and could enjoy the festivities.

Two days later the ship docked in Halifax, Nova Scotia to disembark some passengers, before going on to New York Harbor. While passengers were getting off the ship, Maris like some other people took advantage of the situation and cast a line down the other side to catch a few fish. He caught some white fish. I have no idea how he got or made a fishing pole, or what was done with the fish. There was no way we could cook it.

On December 28, 1950 the General Taylor slid past the Statue of Liberty in the night and we did not get to see her until daylight broke and the harbor lights disappeared.

> *Give me your tired, your poor*
> *Your huddled masses*
> *Yearning to be free ... (Emma Lazarus)*

In the night we had also passed a place called Ellis Island. Mother was so thankful that we were not pulled off the ship on Ellis Island. It sounded like a prison sentence to me, a place we would never get out of. This was her biggest fear throughout the entire crossing, unlike my fears, "Will the boat stay afloat all the way across?" One day later I would find out why she had these fears. My stepsister had been exposed to the chicken pox just 21 days earlier. Before getting off the ship all the Lutheran sponsored immigrants were given a green pin-on button with three white letters on it—LWF, which stood for Lutheran World Federation. I wore mine proudly, and felt important. Such vanity!

We disembarked and waited for our boxes to be unloaded. Arvids took care of all that. It was an all day wait. The port was large and had plenty of seating. On the left side where we sat were large dirty windows that went practically from ceiling to floor. What a place this was—this new world! So much going on! It sure was a fast paced world here, and I didn't know how I could survive in a place like this. It was not appealing. Buildings and more buildings and very tall buildings; a sight I had never seen before. Some buildings were so tall that it made me dizzy to look at the top of them. I saw many streets and bridges that didn't even cross water, just other streets. Cars, so many cars! They went flying by the huge windows like racing dogs, all day long without ever letting up. I wondered where so many people could possibly be going, and why were they in such a hurry? What would happen if they crashed into each other? Then I started to look for Rudy in the cars. I knew he had a car but not what it looked like. And I knew he lived nearby, actually in Newark, New Jersey! I never did spot him, but I tried.

The day seemed to last forever. I became very hungry and so were the others. This time there were no sacks of dried bread ends or smoked fish. The day wore on. No concession stands were anywhere to be found, and none of us were about to venture out on the street in a strange land to find food without American dollars.

"My first day in America and I went hungry all day," I thought. Somehow it wasn't what I expected.

By early evening we had connected with the train that would take us first into Philadelphia, then to Williamsport. Yes, at that time, 1950, the passenger trains were still running in Williamsport. It is now called Little League Boulevard and the train tracks are gone. The iron monolith came to a screeching halt near High Street. The little train station was closed because it was 3:00 AM. We were to get off here and meet with some of the parishioners who had driven about 40 miles to meet us in the middle of the night. Three men and two cars were waiting for us in the dark of the night. Reverend Klinger introduced himself first, and then he introduced Verus Krotzer and Walter Krotzer. We had never met or seen them before and visa-versa. Somehow we just knew that we were looking for each other. No other passengers detrained. Our boxes were moved to the baggage area of the small station and we climbed into the two cars to head up the mountain to Liberty. I was in the back seat with my little half-sisters and Mother was up front with Rev. Klinger. We had never ridden in a car before and the experience was another new one for us. The little girls sat on the edge of the back seat trying to see up over the front seats. I don't know what they were thinking since they never uttered a sound. The road was long, narrow and winding. It seemed to take forever as the car continued to climb the mountain.

Arvids and Maris were in the other car with the Krotzer men. Rev. Klinger pulled off the road and stopped in front of one of his four churches, Friedens. He beckoned us to come inside as he went in turning on the lights. I couldn't figure out why we had to see this church before we could sleep for the night, but the Reverend must have thought it was important. I understood so very little except eat and sleep. A few moments later we were back in the cars and at Crissy and Robert Wheeland's home on a farm. At 4:00 AM, Crissy had set the table with white linens and her best china and had small sandwiches and cookies served with tea. We munched on the goodies and sipped on some tea, but most of all we wanted to sleep. Crissy took us upstairs and showed us our respective rooms. This was a big house and we did not have to bunch up to sleep. I had my very own bedroom. I cuddled in the warm clean blankets and sheets and then off to dreamland in no time. The next morning I got a glimpse of the beauty outside. I could see rolling hills blanketed with a thick layer of snow. Outside my window were four blue spruce trees, their branches laden with a coating of snow.

December 29, 1950, right on cue, my half sister woke up with the chicken pox. It seems like God had spared us from exile on Ellis Island. It is in His time and on His day that things will happen. It is destiny! Twenty-one days later our youngest sibling came down with the chicken pox. Maris and I had already been through it, so we were not affected. On the same date, somebody drove to the train station with a pick up truck to get our boxes.

On January 3, 1951, Maris and I were sent to school. Crissy made us each a brown bag lunch and a big yellow bus stopped outside the house and we rolled on to a new school in a language we could not understand or speak. Not knowing much about these school buses, I was the last one on, letting Maris go first. Then I tried to do something very dumb, close the door on the bus! It would not budge. The driver was trying to tell me something but I had no clue what. I just continued to struggle with that bus door until the driver motioned with his hand to come on and go sit down. There was laughter on the bus and I knew it was on me. What are you "gonna" do with an immigrant kid in a strange land who doesn't understand anything?

Maris, Arvids, Laima, Baiba, and the darling little sisters at our first Christmas in our own house in Liberty

11

Life in America

We stayed at Crissy's house for about two weeks and then were taken to our own little place back in the woods on a dirt road. It was a cute little dwelling that had a habit of looking like a gingerbread house. The three front stained glass windows gave it that special charm. The house had four rooms, two downstairs and two upstairs with an open stairway. No indoor plumbing. We pumped the water from a hand pump outside and used an outhouse for the obvious purposes. The kitchen was heated with a cook stove and the living room with a wood stove. Whatever heat radiated upstairs gave us some comfort for the night.

The special people of the Liberty Valley Lutheran Parish had furnished the little house with antique like furniture, with all the kitchenwares, towels, clothing and bedding. The Ladies Aid made a couple of crazy quilts that had each lady's name embroidered on it. They gave us everything we needed to set up housekeeping again. We were very grateful for all of these blessings. Pastor Klinger came to visit often and so did other parishioners. They always brought us something. What I wanted most of all were cakes, cookies, puddings, pears, and most any kind of sweets. Now that sugar was easily available at the local grocery store down town, it was easier for mother to bake some goodies. Since we did not have transportation, we walked everywhere we needed to go, including to church on Sunday and to the downtown Liberty grocery stores. In the beginning there actually were three grocery stores in Liberty. One was owned and operated by Cledas Smith and was on main street. It was more like a general store. His wife worked by his side tenderly and continually. Whenever I had a few cents, I went to the Smiths' store for candy. I bought Tootsie Rolls when they were still four inches long and cost a penny each. My favorite, however, were Mary Jane candies, also a penny apiece. Francis Roupp owned and operated the second grocery store. He and his wife lived in the biggest, most beautiful Victorian house in Liberty. It is still number one on my list and is now owned by the Geisingers. Bob Brion took a bold move in the 1950's and opened a third grocery store in a Victorian house located in the center of town. The store is just across the street from where it started out. It is now the only grocery store in Liberty.

Arvids walked the two miles to the Wheeland Lumber Mill and back every day regardless of the weather. Maris and I walked to school and back every day too, since the bus did not go past the cute little house on the dirt road. We walked to the store and back carrying paper grocery bags. On occasion, Rev. Klinger would come and pick us up for church if the weather was extremely nasty.

School was like being whirled into another world. That first day at school was incredibly surreal. If there were thirty-two kids in the room, of fourth and fifth graders, then sixty-four eyes were on me all day! I sure was an odd ball! I wanted to disappear into the floor somehow or look normal or understand what was going on. I looked strange, with my two long blonde pigtails with big white ribbons tied on the end of each. I wore a long sleeve woolen dress and brown cotton stockings. On my feet I wore brown oxfords. The other girls all wore pretty cotton dresses with white ankle socks and black paten leather shoes. Their hair was mostly short and curly.

I had finished the fourth grade in Gmund and started the fifth grade, but the administrator, Mr. Anderson, and teachers decided that I should be put into the fifth grade that I was probably behind in academics, having missed three months of school during the immigration process. My teacher was Mrs. Erway. Maris was placed in the 6th grade and was in Mrs. Brion's room, which, was to the right as you entered the building. She taught grades six, seven and eight.

The three-room schoolhouse stood stoic and proud on a high embankment. It had a wide hallway in the middle and double doors at the entrance that was at the top of five wide concrete steps. The left side housed grades one, two and three and the teacher was Mrs. Taber, a wonderful, sweet as milk chocolate person, who could get those little kids learning phonics and reading with gusto. All the desks and benches were bolted to the floor in all three rooms, but the desks in Mrs. Taber's room were much smaller in size.

Mrs. Erway's room was the largest of the three rooms, at the end of the wide hallway. The desk part and the bench in front of it were one piece. Each desk was made for two students. The top of the desk lifted up to hold books and supplies. My desk was close to the back of the room. Behind all the desks was a long wooden table where we could sometimes play games if our work was finished. *Pick-up sticks* and *Jacks* were the favorite games when we had to be inside. Outside we played on the swing set. Some of the girls liked to hang upside down on the hand bars by their knees and let their pretty white cotton underwear show. The boys didn't pay much attention, but I thought it was terribly embarrassing.

The teacher never had to go outside with us. Except for the day two boys got into a fight, there really were no problems.

Mr. Anderson came in once in awhile to see how I was doing. One time I understood Mrs. Erway say to him, "She's good in arithmetic, but she can't read English." Yeah right, I didn't even know how to ask where the bathroom was! Indeed, I was good at arithmetic since I could do all four operations with fractions by the time I had finished fourth grade in Gmund. Here the students were just starting fractions in fifth grade.

Liberty High School was housed over what later became known as the bank building and all classes were on the second and third floors. The gym and cafeteria were in the building that became known as the community hall. Mr. Anderson had his office in the high school. Sometimes we had hot lunches in the community hall basement but that was only in the winter. The building is now a church.

The first week I was in the school, two things happened. First, Mary Jean gave me a doll with eyes that opened and closed and all dressed in pink. She had a cloth body, rubber-like soft arms and legs and a porcelain head. She was the most beautiful doll I had ever held in my arms and it was love at first sight. My very first doll!

The other thing that happened that same week was that everyone had to do a book report, including me. Well, I picked out a book that I thought looked interesting and pretended to read it. On the book report, we had to fill out the names of the characters, which was easy enough to catch by the use of capital letters. I think I was also able to pick out the location of the story, again by use of capital letters and a time period. When it came to writing the summary, I was stuck. So, I did the next best thing. I took one paragraph from the book that looked interesting and copied it word for word as the summary. I drew a picture from the book and handed it in, quite proud of my accomplishment.

The next day the book reports were handed back and Mrs. Erway was not too pleased with mine.

"You can't copy a paragraph from the book and use it as a summary!" she scolded. At the same time I'm thinking, "What's a summary?"

However, this did not discourage me from reading. Then I became extremely homesick, a feeling I had never experienced. I couldn't eat, I couldn't smile, and I didn't talk. I was sad everyday. I wanted to go back to Scwhabisch Gmund, where my friends and familiar places were; a place where I could understand the language. What made things worse is that the camp in Gmund, no longer existed. Everybody had been dispersed to a new location. It was a very desperate feeling being so homesick for something that was no more.

In April came the Scholastic Achievement Tests. I scored high in the math part but in the reading part I didn't even come close to passing. Many questions were about Nursery Rhymes and American Folk Tales, which of course, do not exist in Latvian Literature. Reading in English was still the biggest challenge. After considering my lack of language ability, it was decided that I would be placed in fifth grade again next year.

Spring came and Arvids prepared a plot to plant a garden. He started seedlings in the house and the plants would have a head start. Maris cleared the blackberry bushes to make room for a garden. Arvids planted a big garden and fenced it in with chicken wire for keeping the chickens out of it. He purchased chicks and we kept them in the house until they were old enough to go outside in the shed. One day everybody went away and I was left to watch that the chickens didn't get in the garden patch. I was sternly reminded that if the chickens get in the garden, they would destroy all the tender little plants. They could easily fly up and go over the fence into the garden where the soil was soft and easy to scratch about for some delicious bugs and worms. I watched that garden like a hawk. Then it started to rain and I knew that chickens usually take cover from the rain and go in the coop, so I didn't have to worry about them. Wrong! I curled up with the book I was reading and became lost in the story.

I got up to look out the window to see if it was still raining and it was. Then I glanced at the garden. To my horror, I saw every chicken in the garden scratching and picking! It was still raining, but I had not realized that chickens would take cover only if it is a hard rain. When it rains lightly, it is the best time for digging and scratching.

"What do I do now? I am in big trouble for sure!"

I started to yell and scream and chase the chickens out of the garden. Then I shut the chicken coop door like I should have in the first place. When I saw the cucumber plants all dug up I started to bawl. The tomato plants were lying here and there and everywhere. Still sobbing, I watched the driveway for them to come walking in and me catching the punishment. As the rain kept lightly falling, I carefully replanted everything that was dug up, but I was sure the cucumber plants would not make it, because once you disturb their roots, they are done. I left everything in the garden looking as normal as it did and just maybe Arvids would not notice. I was safely back in the house and in dry clothes when they came home. I did not say a word about the garden or the chickens.

The next day Arvids asked me if the chickens were in the garden while he and the rest of them were away. I said, "Yeah, a couple of them." To my delight, all the cucumbers survived the upheaval, and so did I. Thank you Lord!

Then there was the rooster. The rooster was kept for fertilizing the eggs so the hens could hatch chicks. This rooster was kind of cocky and among other things, mean. I could always get away from him or grab a stick and run after him. But my younger little sibling was only four when the rooster flew on her back and started pecking her on the back of the head and neck. She was running through the yard screaming, trying to get away from him. I was scared too because the rooster could really hurt her. I went after that rooster with the biggest stick I could grab. That was the end of Mr. Cocky Rooster. He lost his head soon after that, and Mother roasted the rooster for our dinner roster!

In August we enjoyed delicious bright red, perfectly shaped tomatoes and loads of succulent cucumbers among other garden vegetables. Mother pickled the small cucumbers in a crock with dill and salt. We also had lots of cabbage and cauliflower. The food shortage in our lives was in the past now as we enjoyed the bounty of our new land.

Some pigeons had taken up residence in one of the sheds. Maris and I were fascinated with them and wanted to see if they really could send messages. We never figured out how to do that but we did clip the wings on one of them to see if he would stick around. Yep, he did, and Arvids was not happy with our actions. A few years later Maris dropped a cat out of the second floor barn window, just to see if it would land on his feet! Yep, he did, but I was upset this time, because I felt sorry for the cat.

Maris dragged an old bicycle home one day and fixed it up. We both rode it even though it was a boy's bike. He went to Wheeland's a lot so he really needed it more than I did. He did odd jobs for them and earned a little spending money, which he mostly spent on food and snack items, and of course, bicycle parts. Then he moved in with Crissy and Robert to help milk the cows and other farm work. He went to school from the Wheelands and rode the bus. I continued to walk to school and back up the dirt road to the little house. As I was walking home one day, a boy jumped out of the bushes and put his arm around me and acted like he wanted to kiss me. I got about as inflexible as a terrified cat with its back humped up. He sensed my fright after awhile, I guess, and let go of my waist and ran on ahead to his home. I am just **so** not ready for this!

From then on, I was afraid to walk up the dirt road, and decided to take a shortcut through the fields. This strategy if it worked would bring me out right in front of the house by cutting across the fields diagonally. It seemed like a long walk, and for awhile I was afraid I was lost. But I kept trudging on when suddenly in front of me is the little house in the woods with the stained glass windows in the front. My strategy had worked!

I did not take the field route again because it was too difficult to walk through the tall grass and the round, dark brown pancake mounds that ruled the meadows, not to mention climbing all those fences. But still I had fears about somebody jumping out of the bushes at me when I walked up the dirt road. And if that wasn't enough, the people at the top of the dirt road had two German shepherd dogs that always came to chase me and bark at me. The dogs never listened to their owners and did their own thing. The owners said that if I didn't run, the dogs probably wouldn't chase me. Sure, did I really want to find out? However, the dogs never did anything more than just scare me badly.

We had been in America just about six months, when I attended my first church picnic. It was held in downtown Liberty at the ballpark. Every family that came brought a dish to pass and their own table service. A pavilion with long rugged picnic tables provided the picnic atmosphere at the ballpark. The pavilion and the picnic tables still stand and are used today. The women set the food dishes in the middle of the picnic tables. Finally everyone sat down to feast, but only after the Reverend had given the table grace. The food dishes started going from person to person all the way around all the tables. The food was so foreign looking to me that I let everything go by and sent it on to the next person. Somebody curiously asked me why I wasn't putting anything on my plate?

"I'm waiting for the good stuff!" I replied, meaning the deserts. I had a way of sticking my foot in my mouth a lot.

In September my half-sister started first grade. I walked with her but in the opposite direction that I had always walked. It was a shorter walk to the East Point hard road where the school bus would pick us up. Maris always went his own way on the bicycle. I liked this arrangement much better since I didn't have to go past the dogs or worry about someone jumping out of the bushes!

Our second winter in the little house was coming to a close. Arvids and Mother talked about buying some property and remaining in Liberty. Our lease agreement with the church would soon be up, and we needed to move on. In God's kingdom, everything happens at the right time, in the right place, and the puzzle to our wandering years was finally coming together.

Francis Neal, owner of a feed mill and loyal Liberty Lutheran member, had a place in mind. The farm was on top of Jew Hill. It would be ideal for Arvids to start his greenhouse business: with eight acres of tillable land; a big two story farmhouse; a two story horse barn with two horse stalls; a long chicken coop; and a pig shed. All of the buildings were old and needed some work. The hand pump was just outside the kitchen and the outhouse about 15 feet away towards the back of the house. The deal was made with the owner and Mr. Neal bought it for $3000. He sold the house to Arvids @ $300 per year for ten years. Arvids had the house paid off in less than the three years time. Arvids took a job at the Blossburg Foundry working evenings and nights. At first he had to rely on a neighbor who also worked the same shift, for transportation. Then Arvids bought the first family car, a 1940 Chevrolet coop, a boring gray color. Arvids took very good care of the old car and kept it in the barn. Maris was the only person in the family with a driver's license and drove Mother or Arvids where they needed to go and also drove it to school.

The year was 1952 and we had no indoor plumbing. Then there came a day when Maris drove Mother and Arvids to Williamsport where they bought a bathroom set; tub, sink, and toilet at Sears and Roebuck. It was sky blue and very pretty. Two more years would go by before there was running water and a flushing toilet in the house. The blue commodity sat in the barn until Arvids had time to install all that was necessary to have a working bathroom. The bathroom was finally installed in the room just off the kitchen that was once a pantry. The walls were painted blue and linoleum was placed over top of the old floorboards. Arvids put in a cesspool just outside the bathroom as it was just far enough away from the well. There were no codes to abide by back then.

The house had five bedrooms upstairs with one small hall closet. The master bedroom was large, had a balcony with a roof and four windows. My room was in the front of the house and had three windows. I picked out wallpaper of yellow roses and it was the most beautiful room in the whole house. Yellow roses were Arvids favorite flowers. He would come and stand in my doorway and just silently admire this room. He also built a wardrobe in each bedroom using curtains for the doors. Each of us kids had our own bedroom now, such a luxury! It wasn't long before I had my walls pinned with all kinds of movie star pictures cut out of magazines. Arvids said it was a shame to cover up all those beautiful roses. But I had dreams in my head.

I learned years later that my sisters had a lot of fun with my clothes closet. They liked to dress up and put on my high-heeled shoes and have a great time. I could tell that my clothes were not the way I had left them and confronted my sisters. After that they got very crafty. They wrote down the order of the clothes and the shoes so they could put everything back the way I left them. I never knew the difference!

Downstairs had a huge living room, two other small rooms and a large kitchen with two huge overly painted, white dry-sinks. They had been painted so many times that the doors would not shut all the way.

When we first moved in, our source of heat was by wood stoves that had smoke pipes running through the upstairs bedrooms and on through the chimneys on the roof. In the kitchen Mr. Neal brought his mother's **Majestic** cook stove. It made the kitchen nice and cozy in the winter. All of the stoves were fired by slab wood, so Maris and I had a lot of wood stacking to do. In back of the kitchen was like a woodshed to keep the wood dry and out of the snow for winter. Maris and I stacked a lot of wood in there too. As unbelievable as it may sound, I actually liked stacking the wood, just to see how straight I could do the ends.

We took our baths in the kitchen in an oval galvanized tub with water that was heated on the cook stove. It was just big enough for one small person sitting with bent knees. An old cast iron sink was already in the kitchen that had a drain. When Rudy was visiting us, as he did from time to time, the hand pump broke, so Arvids installed pipes from the well to the sink. Maris dug the well pit and helped Arvids install an electric articulating pump. At least we had cold running water then.

Maris helped Arvids build the first greenhouses. He made all the necessary wood rafters and wall sections in the barn, and built all twelve windows by hand in the upstairs master bedroom; it was a large room and empty at that time. He cut the wood pieces with a hand saw in the barn and then assembled them in the upstairs room. All the windows were pegged and glued and were placed on the half greenhouse against the chicken coop. Then Arvids built a foundation and frame for the first freestanding, full sized greenhouse, using the windows that Maris made just as the ones for the little greenhouse. Both greenhouses went together like a prefab house would today.

The next part of this story, I wish I didn't have to write. But to free myself, I must tell it. "And you shall know the truth, and the truth will set you free." (John 8:32)

One thing all of us enjoyed was swimming in the summer. No, we were not used to swimming pools, but the creek was very welcoming on hot summer days or evenings. A church friend would come by and load us kids in his car and take us to the Roaring Branch Creek to swim. Since I didn't have a swimming suit, I would wear a white T-shirt and a pair of shorts. Seeing me in a wet tee, (no training bra, never knew they existed) the church friend made comments to me how good I looked in my wet tee. I felt totally awkward about the comment as I did not have a positive attitude about my body and did not like anybody noticing it, let alone a grown man. It would only be the beginning of the saga that I would somehow like to forget!

I was asked to baby sit for the church friend's kids. I did this on many occasions. I also mowed lawn for them and so earned a little spending money to buy clothes and music. I had just turned thirteen. When his wife was in the hospital, I was asked to stay with the children. I had the kids in bed when the man came home. To my horror he moved really close to me, took my hand and asked me to let him love me. He told me I was pretty. Terribly frightened, I broke away from him and ran into the bathroom and locked the door. He stood outside the door and begged me to unlock the door. He said he wouldn't hurt me, but just wanted to love me. I kept saying, "No, no, no …" I climbed in the tub and sobbed quietly and repeated, "No, leave me alone, I don't want to …" he begged and pleaded on for at least an hour or more. I knew this would be a long night, but there was no way I was coming out of the bathroom. Then he offered to give me $100 if I would do it with him. Here I am sitting in a tub, shaking like a leaf, every nerve end on alert, sobbing, trapped, and alone, pondering how I was ever going to get out of this situation. To my relief, he finally gave up and said he was going to leave me alone and go to bed. Still very much afraid, I stayed in the tub all night sleeping on some towels. Early in the morning, I made my escape from the bathroom very quietly and ran home as fast as my feet could carry me. Dawn was just breaking through the night sky.

I did not mention this incident to anyone because somehow, I thought I had done something wrong. Or what is wrong with me, that I'm being treated this way. "Mother would never believe me that a decent church person would even think about treating a child like that. They are all good people here and they have helped us a lot. Don't start any rumors about anyone here," I imagined her saying to me.

The harassment did not stop. He was after me every chance he could find. One day he wanted to teach me how to drive a car. I got in the driver's seat and he told me to drive way back in the hayfield. He praised my driving skills and again made motions to convince me that I need to know about lovemaking. Scared and embarrassed, I stopped the car and jumped out and again ran home. Why is this happening? Why? Why? Why? What is wrong with me that a man old enough to be my father lusts after me? I was not beautiful, or sexy, or have a nice body. My body was still frail and skinny, but I had started to develop my breasts and felt very self-conscious of them, actually ashamed. He told me off-color jokes, that I didn't understand and on and on. He was always looking at me in a way I did not like, that made me very uncomfortable. I did not know how to handle the situation or how to react.

Some weeks went by when I was asked to mow the lawn and pull weeds from the garden at his house. He came up to me and said he wanted to show me something in the barn. I willingly, trustingly went to the upper part of the barn where the hay is kept. Next thing I know I am on the barn floor, he is on top of me holding me down and ripping my underwear off. As usual I was wearing a dress that day. I can't tell you how weird I felt, or how horrible it was. I was confused, afraid and helpless! I could do nothing but scream for help as loud as I could. I yelled his wife's name and screamed help some more. But no one heard me. He told me to shut up, that he didn't want his wife to come out here. He pursued his pleasure on his scrawny captive. When it was over, I pulled my underwear back up and awkwardly took off for home. My self-concept hit rock bottom. I felt weird, guilty, ashamed, dirty, thinking it was entirely my fault. I must be doing something wrong. I told no one and for many years went into denial that it ever happened.

A young kid of thirteen should not have to worry about being pregnant, even though my period had not fully started previous to the ordeal, but the thought was in my mind constantly until enough time passed to negate those thoughts. I kept the secret to myself. The man has passed away and I have no closure. I have to go on with life.

Years later I became angry about the tribulation. How could he even think about something this indecent against a young girl? I was just a kid! I knew nothing about sex nor wanted to know. I had never even seen male genitals. Had I somehow asked for this? I was robbed of my childhood by the war years and now robbed of a very sacred part of my own person, my self-respect! I was terribly violated and I was still a child. He was after all, a church pillar, a husband and father. I kept the anger inside. The ordeal followed me into my marriage and in time that failed too. I did not mention it to my then husband. I figured he might react with jealousy and make me feel cheap. I am still angry and have blamed the horrendous act for my lack of a meaningful relationship with any male ever. The guilt must have started to work on the church friend some years later. I was in my fifties when he sent me a traveler's check of a sizeable amount as if to pay penance, to repair the damage done. Rape is something you cannot repair! It stays with you forever. There is no erasure or compensation when it comes from your flesh. I kept the secret to myself for fifty some years. I never, ever mentioned the incident to the man either. My self-concept is expressed in the following excerpt:

"There wasn't anything about me or going for me that would make someone want me or want to be with me, much less listen to me. I was not beautiful. My body was ugly. People would turn away from me. I wore remade clothes. I was poor. I was laughed at by my peers and shunned by those older than myself."*

*From On the Threshold of Hope, Diane M. Langberg, used by permission.

Meanwhile back at the farm on Jew Hill, in early spring, Arvids started his seedlings and by March we spent most of our time in the greenhouses transplanting the little darlings into flats and six packs to sell later. Petunias took the longest to grow, so they were started and transplanted first. Then arrived the time to transplant all the cabbage family veggies; and the flowers—ageratum, marigolds, zinnias, and fuchsias, etc. The last to be transplanted were the tomato plants. We transplanted until the end of the selling season in June. All greenhouses in the spring portray greenness and the all flowers are in bloom. A breath taking sight!

When it was cabbage-planting time, I joked with Mother that we should start a cabbage planters' union so we could go on strike. We had a lot of fun while we transplanted cabbage. Arvids prepared the field and made rows, and then he showed Maris and me how to plant the cabbage. Mother would walk along the rows and drop the cabbage plant and I would cover the roots with the soil and Maris came along with the watering can and gave them water. We did the whole field in the front by the road like that. It was probably about a half of an acre or so. When the cabbage was planted, we did the same with the tomatoes. In August, Maris borrowed Wheeland's truck and with Arvids took cabbage, tomatoes and cucumbers to Williamsport to the supermarkets. The very first load was only cabbage. They sold well and were beautiful vegetables. Then a law was passed that supermarkets had to get their produce from unionized growers and Arvids could no longer sell his fantastic vegetables in Williamsport. From then on we planted enough cabbage to make a barrel of sauerkraut for our own use. We all liked sauerkraut especially the way Mother made it.

What I enjoyed most about life was school. The new high school had just been built so now the seventh grade students went to the high school, The Liberty Joint Jr.-Sr. High School. By the time I was in the seventh grade, I had all A's on my report card. Mr. Anderson again talked it over with the teachers and they together decided that a mistake had been made in placing me in the fourth grade twice. Once I cracked the language, I really excelled in the academics. The summer after I finished the seventh grade, Mr. Anderson hired a teacher, Mrs. Brion, to tutor me all summer so I could skip eighth grade and be promoted to the ninth grade by September. This was a tremendous boost to me and I still continued to get straight A's. At graduation, I was nineteen. Had it not been for Mrs. Brion, I would have been twenty!

I also went to church and Sunday School every Sunday; Rev. Klinger's rules! But I certainly did enjoy it! I sang in the youth choir and participated in Catechism Class for two years and then was confirmed in the Liberty Lutheran Church. It did not seem like a big deal to anyone but me. I received no flowers like Tuta did at her confirmation. But I finally had my pure white dress, a brand new dotted swiss store bought dress. As a matter of fact I had a lot of very nice dresses. The Neals' daughter, Mary Louise, was just a little older than I was and being the only child had beautiful clothes. Mrs. Neal gave me all of Mary Louise's outgrown clothes. Then she took me to a hairdresser and had my hair cut and styled. It really did look nice, but I just wasn't used to loose hair or working with it. Mary Louise gave me piano lessons every week. I truly enjoyed the attention I was getting, and this was strictly only for me.

I was into glamour with my new clothes, new hairdo. Then I decided to paint my fingernails. Wow! Glamour galore! When Arvids saw my nails, he made me go and take the color off. I pleaded that my younger siblings had nail polish on and she was only six! He said she doesn't know what it means, but on me painted nails looked cheap! From then on I only wore nail polish when he wasn't around. When I had saved up enough money I bought a little fuzzy white spring jacket and felt like a movie star. Marilyn Monroe. I was so proud to have it and happy that I could feel this good about myself. But when Arvids saw it, he said it was too good for me and the other girls downtown didn't have a jacket that nice so I couldn't have one either. After all, I was not supposed to outshine the townspeople or their daughters who helped us get here. He said I had to take the coat back. I went to my bedroom and cried a bushel of tears. I decided that I was not worthy of anything nice. Mother, my angel, came up and told me softly that I didn't have to take the coat back but not to wear it in front of Arvids and everything would be alright. I felt better, but it was difficult to sneak the coat out the door. I could not understand why I was not worthy of anything nice.

I worked as hard as I was asked to work, and did well in school. To drown my sorrows, I read books without ceasing. I could forget my troubles and lose myself in the books I read. It was my escape from reality just as fantasizing got me through childhood. Tom Sawyer, Huck Finn, Caddie Woodlawn, and many others became my friends. I read books in Latvian and in English. *Rulamans* was my favorite book in Latvian. A few months ago, I found the book at my half-sister's house and she said I should have it. Eagerly I put it in my suitcase. I had discovered a lost treasure! It now sits on my bookcases in the study. The book was about an early cave man society that was destroyed by the enemy of time and was no more. I identified my situation with this group as the Latvian society we had in Germany that also was no more; destroyed by destiny. I felt so bad about the book's ending that I could not eat my supper that night.

My confirmation day

Lilita and me

12

The Air Force Beckons

Maris' fascination with airplanes during the war propelled him into the air force later. He thought it was safer to be in the airplane in the sky rather than to be shot at on the ground. One could tell his interest was in mechanics judging by the pictures of motors and spark plugs he had glued on the headboard of his antique bed.

While in high school Maris dated a girl named Patsy Knipe. She was the only child in her family and lived on a dairy farm. The relationship did not last and they went their separate ways. Much later in life Patsy would be in the picture again. Maris played center on the Liberty High School basketball team; he was an ace. He also played soccer and intramural baseball. He excelled as a student, and hardly had to study. In the high school musicals, he usually played the lead male role since he had a great voice. He seemed to be good at most everything. Like I said in the beginning, he was very smart.

Maris was a big help to Arvids in and around the greenhouses. He helped build, plant, fix and mix. Maris was his right hand man. When he got his car, it was harder to keep him down at the greenhouses. He turned sixteen in June of 1953 and was freewheeling. He drove his friends around since none of them had a car, and went who knows where with his buddies. This freewheeling caused a lot of friction between Maris and Arvids. It was a constant battle between the two. He, in 1956, decided to go on his own and discover the world.

In 1956 Maris left home before his senior year in high school, due to age restrictions in high school sports programs and joined the Air Force. He was mature and very capable. He did his basic training at Lackland Air Force Base in Texas for eleven weeks. From there he was sent to Wichita Falls also in Texas for tech school and trained in aircraft repair. While there he earned his GED without much effort. His first overseas duty was in Guam to repair aircraft. When the Air Force personnel realized he was not an American citizen, he was not allowed to work on airplanes. He applied for citizenship papers immediately and while waiting worked in the administration office for the Strategic Air Command. He was in Guam from December 1956 until March 1958.

Between assignments, he came home for a couple weeks and married a hometown girl from Nauvoo. They moved to Utah where he was stationed for four years and was on secret mission. They had three children: a girl Lori and two boys, Lester and Leonard. The marriage didn't work out and they were divorced.

Next he was stationed in Oklahoma City, the training base for flight engineer school for C-124 planes. He was stationed permanently at McChord Air Force Base, but went back to Oklahoma City once more for flight training school.

While Maris was stationed at McChord Air Force Base for the rest of his Military career, he flew in and out of Vietnam missions for combat duty from 1965–1968. Each mission was considered a combat mission, however, due to the politics of the Vietnam era, the military personnel were considered expendable. It was more important to please the press than to protect the military. The persons flying in and out of war zone were required to spend five days in combat, before they were considered for a combat mission. This practice all changed when one of the flight crew was shot and killed by a sniper, that the five-day restriction was removed. The "TET" offensive in 1968 was proof of United States military supremacy, since the North Vietnamese military was defeated. At that time the politicians decided to stop all aggression, which allowed the enemy to recoup.

He met and married a German woman (with a strong German accent) who was slightly older than he was. She owned a cute little bungalow in Tacoma and worked in the local PX. She had three children but only the youngest one was still at home and in high school. I had my doubts about her from the very beginning. She was constantly at Maris about things he did and things he didn't do. She was moody and a chain smoker, but wanted very much to show us that she was a good German. Every morning, she would sit in bed and have that cigarette before she could get up. She cooked some really wonderful German dishes; Bratwurst; German potato salad; Roladen and much more. She took us to German cafes and we treated ourselves with German tortes.

In 1968 he was discharged from the Air Force on disability. He then worked in the Veterans' Administration Regional Office as benefits counselor. He always thought about getting a college degree. In 1980 he started taking courses at Pacific Lutheran University, attending evening classes. In 1989 he graduated with a Bachelor of Arts degree in Sociology. Now, all four of us kids have a college degree.

Western Washington State has a high concentration of German population. There are many restaurants and cafes, beer gardens and bistros. Oktoberfest was celebrated with lots of food and beer. The weather was always temperate, lots of rain and very little snow. When Mother and I went to see Maris, he met us at the train station. I had not seen him for seven years and was nervous. He enlightened us with a tour of Seattle and the giant Redwood trees. I thought Seattle was the most beautiful and the cleanest city in the United States. With all the flowers and greenery, it reminded me very much of towns in Germany. Actually, the whole state of Washington is very beautiful; even the eastern part with its rolling hills of dry land and super highways is attractive. I also saw the Pacific Ocean for the first time and with my pant legs rolled up, I waded in the chilly waters of this magnificent ocean.

The second Amtrak trip Mother and I took to see Maris was a little more traumatic. His present wife met us at the train station in Tacoma to tell us that Maris was not in Tacoma and had left her. She knew where he was and would take us to Selah, Washington. It was about a three-hour drive to Selah, located on the eastern side of the Cascade Mountains of Washington.

She drove us right to the house where Maris was supposed to be living, but found no one at home. I wrote several notes and posted them on each door and I placed one in the mailbox to be sure he got the message. Then Mother and I went into the apple orchard where we thought he might be working to look for him. We soon found some Mexicans working in the orchard and asked them if they knew where Maris was. They looked puzzled and answered something in Spanish. Then both Mexicans took off on the run away from us and further into the orchard grove.

By this time a huge storm seemed to be approaching. I could see the black clouds and the relentless lightening in the distance. The wind was whirling profusely and blowing dust in swirls all around us. It became difficult to see. Outdoor furniture was blowing around as if a tornado was in process. Surely it would start to pour down rain any minute. We scrambled back into the car quickly and drove to a nearby restaurant named, The Mining Company. It was authentically decorated with unfinished boards and picks and shovels; very realistic. Inside the restaurant, the waiters told us it never rains in Selah; it just acts like it is going to but never does. We had a wonderful meal and when we left the restaurant, there was no sign of a storm or rain. We drove back to the house where Maris was staying but again no one was there. We rode back to Tacoma, in great disappointment. The next day, having found my many messages, he drove to Tacoma to see us.

He went back to Tacoma and to his wife after that. I never asked him what the problem was. Years later after Arvids died, Maris left Tacoma for good and came to Liberty to help Mother run the greenhouse business.

Maris attended Friedens Lutheran church where Mother went. He sang in the choir and so did Patsy Knipe, now Matthews. She had married and the two of them ran her parents' farm. They adopted a girl and a boy in infancy. The kids grew up and had their own lives and then her husband died. Patsy sold the farm and bought a little house nearby. The house had once been the Jackson School, a one-room schoolhouse for all grades. Patsy attended school at Jackson until she was in eighth grade, when she was transferred to Buttonwood for one year. The last four years of school she went to the high school in Liberty, which was housed over the bank building.

The previous owners had remodeled it into a nice little home. Patsy was still near her farm home and could see the farmhouse from her windows. Her daughter lived nearby in a trailer and Patsy was very happy about that.

Patsy and Maris started seeing each other and rekindled the old flame. They decided to get married and had a small but beautiful wedding at the Friedens Church. They lived in the schoolhouse home until her daughter moved to town. Then Patsy decided to sell the little schoolhouse and move to Liberty too. She and Maris bought a house on Main Street in Liberty so she could be close to her daughter and her three grandkids.

Patsy loves animals and they have many birdfeeders outside and two parakeets inside, plus a dog and a cat. Maris is an avid fisherman and goes fishing every opportunity there is. In 2006 he caught the prize-winning fish about thirty-seven inches long and received $1000. He had the fish mounted and then placed it on his wall.

They live quietly in their house in Liberty. Selah.

Patsy and Maris on their wedding day

Maris' 37-inch prize fish

13

Education Endeavors

I loved going to school. It was a place where I could find friends and happiness. I also loved learning; it was very fulfilling. It seemed like there was so much knowledge that I had not learned about. I wanted to know the origins of everything, and details, details, details. By the time I had a good grasp on the English language, school became easy, whether it was reciting a long poem or doing math, and even book reports were fun.

After spending a year and a half in the fifth grade in Mrs. Erway's class, I was promoted to sixth grade and went into Mrs. Brion's class. This is the year I started having nosebleeds every day. I was in the back row, too close to heater and asked Mrs. Brion if I could be moved to a seat closer to the front. I was probably in the back because of my excellent behavior. (LOL) The nose bleeds continued anyway. Then I asked to be moved to the second seat from the front and now I was right behind John, a boy I liked. The nosebleeds did not stop, but Mrs. Brion caught on to my manipulative ways and moved me to the back of the room once more.

I went to see Dr. Buckley, who lived on Liberty Hill and practiced general medicine. After several visits about my nosebleeds, Dr. Buckley decided to close off the vein in my nose that was causing all the trouble. Soon my nosebleeds stopped altogether.

Dr. Buckley always told me that he would put the charges on my mother's bill. I asked her one day about the doctor's account, "Dr. Buckley has never charged us for his health services. All of the years he was in Liberty, we had his services for free." Wow, what an extraordinary man! When Dr. Buckley retired, he and his wife moved away from the Liberty area, otherwise people would still come to him. He died in the 1970's.

When it was time for me to go to the seventh grade, the new Liberty High School had just been finished. I am not exactly sure how many students matriculated at the high school including grades seven through twelve. The school was named The Liberty Joint Jr.-Sr. High School. In the seventh grade alone there were sixty students. Each grade had two sections. In the fifties, the dropout rate was very high in a rural school. Only 50% of the students that started seventh grade would go on to graduate. The schoolwork was very easy and I became an "A" student in the first quarter and continued to excel throughout the year.

Our History teacher was Mr. William Anderson. A first year teacher, he liked to make the learning fun. Sometimes he would review the events with us through a game like a spelling bee. He divided the class into two teams and we stood in our places in a line along the wall and the windows. We were reviewing the chapter on Greek history. I read the chapter the night before and at that time had like a photographic mind, I could see the words in my mind on the page as each question was presented. Mr. Anderson asked what war destroyed Athens? I was at the end of the line on my team. One by one each student sat down because nobody knew the answer. Finally, I was the only one left standing.

I said, "The Peloponnesian War."

All the rest of the students sat there with their mouths hanging open and in total unbelief.

Somebody asked, "How did you know that?"

"I read about it last night in our book," I replied.

Some other students complained that they read the chapter too, but didn't see that word. I can still see the word on that page in the history book. It was on the left hand page at the top just above a picture of Athens. I referred the other students to the correct page, so they could see it for themselves. From then on, I was hooked on school!

One day a bunch of girls including me, decided to wear cowboy hats to school. We paraded around the school attracting a lot of attention. Then Mr. Anderson's voice came over the loudspeaker, calling each girl with a cowboy hat to the office. Oh, oh, the fun is over and now it is time "to pay the piper." He very nicely, calmly told us not to have these hats in school. It was not the place to wear them. We were all quite embarrassed, but learned a lesson—not to act on a whim. Mr. Anderson was a very understanding man, but he was strict and you had respect for him. I have always held him in high regards.

I loved all of my classes. In English class, it was all about grammar and I found it very easy. In science class, we went to the lab where Mr. Castle taught us how to use the Bunsen burner and where we did many experiments. European geography was a breeze, since I knew more about Europe than I did about the United States. Math came easy too. So what's not to like?

My favorite, however, was gym class followed very closely by music class. We had gym only twice a week and music three times a week. Let me tell you about the required gym uniforms, which the family had to buy. They were a royal blue, all one piece. They buttoned up in the front, and had a gathered waist plus a buckle in the front. The top had short sleeves and a lapel collar finished the top. The bottom part of the uniform was a like a pair of shorts, but the inside of the legs the material was gathered with elastic. White socks and sneakers finished the outfit. There was no chance of anything showing while we did our maneuvers. A far cry from what I saw when I went to college, where I just happened to notice a young man relaxing in an easy chair in his shorts without any visible underwear and his gonad sticking out! And this was in the library! When it was time for gym, we went to the shower room to change, and then reported to the gym floor where we formed a straight line according to height on the basketball court. Mrs. Taylor, an English teacher, was our gym teacher too. Even though some girls complained, I liked everything she had us do, whether it was tumbling or calisthenics or marching. We learned a lot of things and put on a gym show for the parents at the end of the school year. The bleachers were always full for this occasion. When I was in the tenth grade, our school hired a new gym teacher, Miss Fairchild. She was young, cute and energetic. Everybody liked her very much.

At the end of seventh grade, I had all "A's" on my report card. That was when Mr. Anderson made the decision that I needed to study all summer and be promoted to the ninth grade. I walked down the hill to Liberty five days a week for my lessons with Mrs. Brion. No problem here, I liked learning. In the fall of 1955, I became a freshman at Liberty High and still got all "A's." Mr. Anderson had made the right decision.

While I was still a ninth grader, a kid from Morris asked me to marry him, right away. We had not even dated.

"I want to finish school first," I said.

"You can finish school when you are married too. So how about it?" he pursued.

It was tempting, but I declined. He wasn't my type anyway.

Once, a couple of girls, who were not from the right side of the tracks, asked me to go downtown during school hours and just hang out at the soda shop. Being a naïve fool, reluctantly I said, "Okay."

"But shouldn't we tell Mr. Anderson before we go?" I asked.

"No. He doesn't care if we go. We've done it before," they answered.

Something inside told me this was wrong, but I went anyway. I was excellent in academics, but socially a total idiot. The next day, Mr. Anderson called me into the office before classes began. Again he gently told me that leaving during school hours was not allowed, and that I had taken advice from girls who were not the kind of friends I should trust. I thanked him for his kind advice and never did anything like that again. It seems like I learned my lessons the hard way.

In 1956 I was a junior and still doing very well in my studies. Then everybody started to tell me how this boy, a senior, kept looking at me, like he was interested in me. I told my girlfriends and classmates that I didn't like him; he acted like a mamma's boy. He was, however relentless and finally won me over. His name was Dean. Here was somebody who took an interest in me and really liked me. It was a new experience for me and we started dating. I was seventeen. On our first date, he took me to a campfire gathering at his neighbors', but he didn't tell me it was a campfire party. I thought it was a party and I wore my best dress and white high heels. I felt very much out of place.

Dean graduated from high school in May of 1956, and went on his senior trip to Washington, DC in June. For a graduation gift, I gave him a pair of white socks! On the day of his graduation, we had decided to go to the Pennsylvania Grand Canyon with another couple who were dating. His mother, however, had other ideas and made him stay home and help pick stone from the fields, so they could plant the oats and corn. Instead of looking at the beautiful canyon, all four of us picked stone! After graduation, he stayed on the farm to work for his parents. Then they bought him a car, a 1953 standard shift, green, Chevy sedan.

I continued to study and do well; take part in school musicals; chorus and District Chorus representative; and marched with the band in the percussion section because I did not think I had enough lung power to blow an instrument. Dean and I kept dating. I believed I was really in love. In March of 1957, I became eighteen and we got engaged. When I wasn't going to school or working in the greenhouse, I spent every moment I could with Dean.

In March of 1958, I turned nineteen and graduated in May. I was number five in my class. Had it not been that commercial students were in the competition for valedictorian and salutatorian, I would have been second highest in the academics section. A few years later the commercial students were not included as contenders for top spots. The commercial students have much easier courses. They did not have to take Chemistry or Physics, etc. The only "C" on my report card, which kept me off the honor roll in my senior year, was in typing class. I took it as an elective instead of study hall. I was not then nor am I now very dexterous. I look at the keys when I type. In school the typewriters had blank keyboards. Today, it is much easier to type because of word processing capabilities on the computer.

My graduation night was an exceptionally important event in my life. I proudly marched in my white robe and mortarboard to Pomp and Circumstance in a path that was lined with junior class members dressed in their prom gowns and suits. Then when my name was called, I walked to the podium, shook Mr. Anderson's hand and received my diploma. It was a rewarding moment in my life; an accomplishment. Mother gave me a petticoat for graduation and Dean gave me a Waltham watch. That was big time for me. There was no party or celebration. I did not go to Washington, DC with the class, because Dean did not want me to go, even though I wanted to go very much. I was trying to please him and besides, he promised to take me to Washington some time later. It never happened!

Nobody had mentioned college, and there was no guidance counselor in the high school at that time. I wanted to go but had no idea how to go about it. I started to plan my wedding. Early in the winter, 1958, I bought a pattern and some fine fabric and began to make my wedding dress. The bodice was a sheer nylon with white embroidery. The skirt was floor length with many layers of gathered tulle, better known as nylon net, layered over taffeta. Dean's mother asked me to bring the gown to her house so she could help me sew it. (The first bad omen!) I obliged but ended up sewing most of it myself. When the gown was finished, we took it upstairs and laid it on the bed in the room next to Dean's. (Bad idea!) One day his mother's cat was in the house and was looking for a place to do his job. Yes, you got it; he pooped right on the wedding gown. (The second bad omen!) His mother had managed to clean it up before she told me about the cat.

On June 7, 1958 Dean and I were married. The maid of honor was Sandy. My attendants were Lilita and June. They wore their prom gowns in pink, yellow and blue. Dean's brother Bob was best man and the ushers were two very good friends of Dean, Martin and Cecil. (Cecil took me to my first prom when I was a freshman.) Martin was Dean's first cousin. Dean's mother prepared everything for the entire reception and held the party outside in her back yard. The reception was lovely and the weather was beautiful.

The night before the wedding, I had a dream. In my dream, I was riding in the passenger's seat of a horse drawn buggy. Next to me sat a dirty old man that I had just married. I looked back to see the young man I was supposed to marry and saw him standing on the dirt road looking very forlorn. Both images in the road were that of the man I would marry. (The third bad omen!)

After the wedding, we lived with his parents while building a house on the farm just a stone's throw away from his mother's house. She could watch over us through her kitchen window. In the fall of 1958, we moved into the barely finished house. The outside shell was finished, and we had tarpaper on the roof. The inside walls nothing but studding and insulation; and no ceiling. Not exactly a love nest! An old cook stove was the only source of heat. In the late fifties, some people still believed it was fine to live like pioneers! It was impossible to keep the house warm enough to live in, and we had to move in with his parents again. Six months into the marriage, I realized that life was not any better than when I was still at home. I was determined to make it work and besides I had no place else to go anyway.

Our first baby, Timothy Dean, was a very difficult delivery and he had to be taken with forceps. He weighed seven pounds and eleven ounces. I decided that would be the only baby I would ever have. While I was going under the anesthesia, I felt my heart pounding extremely fast and hard. I saw the tunnel and thought I was leaving this earth. When I awoke, the nurse brought me my newborn. The baby was born with an elongated head, and had instrument marks on each side of his head, but I was too groggy to worry about it. Dean, however, was quite upset about the baby's head shape. In a few days the head went back to normal. When Tim was born, we were again at his mother's, but by late spring the house was more livable. We had a central furnace. This time we moved back in and stayed. By now we had a working toilet, a sink and an old claw-foot tub.

A year later we had our second baby, a girl, born on Lincoln's birthday, February 12. She was very small and weighed in at 6 pounds and 5 ounces. Dean named her Sandy Kay. I was very happy that I had a complete family, a boy and a girl. That would be it for children. I was not going to have any more. Sandy cried a lot both day and night. I got very little sleep and was exhausted. Then we decided to varnish our oak floor in the living room. A very stupid thing to-do, when you have a tiny baby just two months old. She cried more and more every day. She had the diarrhea so bad the morning we were to have her baptized, that we had to call it off until later. I fed her often and she would throw up all the time. The next Sunday, she never stopped crying, and after several hours, her little mouth opened as if crying, but no sound came out. I got very scared that she was going to die, and called for Dean to come so we could take her to the hospital. He was out in the field somewhere tending to a cow that was down. His mother drove down by the field to tell him the baby is sick and that I want her to go to the hospital. He changed his clothes and we got in the car. He checked on the cow again before driving us to the hospital. Then he ripped his good pants crawling through the barb wired fence. The baby had stopped crying and was finally sleeping. She didn't look like anything was the matter with her, if you had not been with her all day. When we arrived at the hospital, the receiving nurses could see no visible sign of a sick baby, but I convinced them she was. When nobody listens is the most helpless feeling.

Sandy Kay was admitted to the hospital and was there for ten days. Three different doctors tended to her and had blood taken from her little toes more than once. They found nothing wrong and sent her home. Again that night she cried and cried. I was up half the night. By morning I was sound asleep.

When I awoke, I heard the words that still ring in my ears, spoken by Dean's mother, "Get her up quick!"

I knew it was not good to hear his mother's voice at six in the morning in our house. Dean had found the baby completely under the blankets when he got up to go milk cows. Right away we thought she had smothered in the blankets. The baby was purplish-blue at my first glance. Dean's mother held the baby as the three of us rushed her out to Dr. Buckley in Liberty. He gave her a shot of adrenalin to get her heart started but it was in vain. She was gone. I went into shock! I could not cry, or talk or think. I could not function. My mind went completely blank for several days. Dr. Buckley assured us that Sandy did not die of suffocation. The little body was taken to the hospital for an autopsy at our request. The death certificate listed the cause of death as "menengo encephalitis," or brain fever. I don't remember much about the funeral except that it was held at Dean's mother's house; a lot of people came to express their sympathy. When I first saw the body in the tiny little white casket, I started screaming and could not stop.

"Her body is so cold!" is all that I could say.

The funeral was on April 25th. After the burial, I walked outside just to be alone for a while. I looked up in the sky, and in the middle of the dark dreary clouds of that day was an opening with rays of sunshine pouring into my soul. I knew this was a sign from God, a promise for something good and wonderful. Thirty-one years later to the date, my first granddaughter was born on April 25th.

After the baby's death, I was deeply depressed and suffered from a lot of back pain. My doctor told me that my uterus had collapsed and I needed abdominal surgery. I still wanted to have a girl, and two years after the surgery I became pregnant and delivered another baby boy. The pregnancy was difficult, but the delivery seemed easier. We named him James Dean. He weighed nine and a half pounds. Jim was more difficult to keep quiet, because he did not have a warm and fuzzy like Tim did. Tim carried around a silky scarf and had his thumb. Jim had neither one. When Jim was three, he had his tonsils removed. Two boys were very nice to have, but I still wanted a girl. Two years later in March, God sent me a little girl. I named her Melanie Lynette, from the Melanie in *Gone with the*

Wind. She weighed a walloping ten pounds. Melanie, like Jim suffered from ton-sillitis and we had hers removed when she was five years old. Now my family was complete and we should live happily ever after. That was not to be.

The war in Europe had ended sixteen years ago, but the battles in my life were ongoing. The Iron Curtain went down in Europe when "the wall" was finished in 1961, separating the Communist controlled countries from free Europe. It was about that time that I started having nightmares about being pregnant and living behind the Iron Curtain. We were trying to escape. I dreamed this same dream over and over. I was pretty nervous that something would happen to Melanie until she was three months old. Then I started to relax.

It was very difficult to get mail through to Latvia or from Latvia. Every letter was censored. Christmas cards were outlawed, but a person from Latvia could send a New Year's card. It was in the early sixties that Mother received a letter from a friend in Bauska that Arvids' mother had died. There was nothing Arvids or Mother could do, but grieve quietly with each other.

I never gave up the idea of going to college. I went to see the high school counselor, that now every high school has. I wanted to be an architect. He talked me out of it, because it was a very competitive field and a college that offers the courses was too far away from my home. He suggested, instead, that I study to be a teacher and attend Mansfield College, just twenty miles away. I took his advice, signed up for the college-board exam and started classes at age twenty-eight in the fall of 1968 when Melanie was two. Even though, both my mother and my mother-in-law tried to talk me out of it, they both helped me out tremendously with the children. Without them I would not have been able to carry out this feat. My husband was supportive all the way.

My biggest college disappointment was getting "C's" in some courses, but then I had a ten-year hiatus from high school graduation. The "new math" phase was in place in all the schools, and I had to relearn the language of math all over again. I had never heard of the "null set" {0} and why do I need one anyway. If you have nothing, you already know that. So what's the big deal?

College was never easy. Literature was my favorite. In my sophomore year, I took Chaucer and Shakespeare in the same semester. Then the next semester I took British Novel, reading a-novel-a-week, and American Literature together. Everyone told me that the sophomore year was the hardest and they were right! The last two years were easier because the courses were mostly all about my major—education. I went for four years but took the summers off to recoup. In the summers I did gardening, canning and freezing vegetables and fruits. And most importantly, I was home with the kids.

In May of 1972, I graduated from Mansfield State College with a Bachelor of Science degree in elementary education. Again, I walked up proudly to the podium when my name was called to receive my diploma. At home that Saturday, I had planned and prepared a graduation party. I invited some friends but mostly family on both sides, but family members came and left at different times during the afternoon. Arvids and Mother couldn't come because they had to be at the greenhouses for plant sales. Other family members didn't come because "Saturday was a busy day." I was very disappointed, but decided that once more my accomplishments did not really matter to others. Dean continued to be very supportive throughout my four years of matriculation.

The following year I did not get a full time job, but did substitute teaching and got a lot of experience. Then in the fall of 1973, I was hired to teach second grade at the Cogan House Elementary School, a part of Southern Tioga School District. After a year of teaching, I went back to Mansfield College to fulfill state requirements and start work on my Master's degree. It took two years of Saturday and evening classes, and I received my diploma for Master of Education. When I finished, I told myself; I would never do college courses again! I was wrong!

For ten years, I taught different subjects and grade levels having moved to the Liberty Elementary School, which was only seven miles from home instead of seventeen. I became the cheerleading coach/advisor. I thoroughly enjoyed that job even though some of the girls were a little difficult. Then I took the job of coaching Jr. Varsity girls' basketball. It was the founding of girls' basketball teams at Liberty High School. Dean was extremely excited about the job and was my paramount assistant. He knew so much more about basketball than I did. We didn't win many games that first year but we learned a lot. We continued the basketball coaching and also worked with the seventh and eighth grade girls on our own time.

By 1976, our marriage was on the rocks. In June our oldest son, Tim graduated from high school and in July I went out west with Mother to visit my brother in Tacoma, Washington. It was my first time to go out west and a beautiful trip it was. We got on the Amtrak train in Harrisburg, Pennsylvania and changed trains in Chicago. Mother was so nervous that she put up a big fuss. She had all of the "what if" questions that I tried to answer reasonably. I finally told her we were only going out west, not to the moon! She finally did settle down, but I think the train rides during the war years came back to her too vividly. I too felt like a refugee once more, and asked for nothing like I was not allowed to do so and accept everything as it was.

The western trains are like first class seats on an airplane. Wide comfortable seats and lots of legroom made for a very pleasant ride. The dining room tables were covered with white linen tablecloths and napkins. The tables were set very elegantly with fresh flowers and beautiful stemware. The waiters were dressed in formal attire and carried a towel on their arm. The food was excellent. The western trains also have domed cars that were on the second floor. From the domed cars, we could see for miles. The rolling hills and gullies all through Montana looked like patchwork quilts for miles and miles. In the far distance we could wee the Rocky Mountains but after traveling all day, they did not appear to get any closer. It was after we had traveled another day that we got a closer look at the sharp, pointed, snow capped Rockies in all their might. The most beautiful scenes were in the Cascade Mountains. The train took us right to Tacoma where Maris met us. I had not seen him for seven years, and he looked very good.

We had a nice visit with Maris and his second wife; saw many sights that included the giant sequoias. I saw the Pacific Ocean for the first time. The beach in Washington State is too cold for swimming or sunning. It was so exciting to see this wonderful country.

On the way back, we took a different route with Amtrak and went to Oakland, California. While at the stop in Oakland, Mother called some Latvian friends who lived in San Francisco. They wanted us to come and visit them and they would drive to Oakland to pick us up. The Amtrak tickets could have the date changed easily. Mother dug in her heels and would not go to Frisco. I was terribly disappointed, since I wanted to see Frisco so badly. When we were back on the train, she explained why she didn't want to go; it was because she had a dreadful fear of the San Francisco Bay Bridge. She was sure it would go down if she were on it. So I never got to see Frisco.

When we were back in Chicago, Mother called Ossi. He came to the train station and then drove us back to his house. Once we wereback in Harrisburg, my husband and kids were waiting for us. It was great to see him again but especially the kids. Because of the long absence, I thought our marriage would work out. Unfortunately, nothing had changed in our relationship and he remained silent and distant.

Then he started not coming home at night. Sometimes he would come home very, very late and crash on the couch and be gone in the morning before I got up. I didn't know where he was or how to get in touch with him. In September I filed for divorce. I never gave up hope that he would come back until on December 26th, when I received the letter from my lawyer that the divorce was final. I was crushed!

The next five years were very difficult. It was hard to make ends meet financially. I had three teenagers in the house and I guess I don't need to say any more about that. The two that were still in school, were involved in a lot of sports activities so I was running with them all the time. It kept me occupied and I had less time to think about my situation. Somehow, I got through it all. When son # 2 graduated from high school, he had enough money saved up to make a down payment on my house; he wanted to remain on the farm and take over his ailing grandfather's farm. A few years later, Jim purchased the farm from his grandmother lock, stock and barrel.

I had a new house built in Liberty on Jew Hill on an acre of land that I bought from my mother. It was a small chalet style house that I designed. Melanie graduated from high school in 1983 and that fall she went off to Mercyhust College in Erie. By this time Tim had joined the Marine Corps and went Parris Island, South Carolina for basic training. I was now totally alone and thought I couldn't wait for the day when I could control the TV and not have to pick up dirty socks. Instead, the worst depression I ever had set in and I couldn't function. I came home from school and became a couch potato and watched M*A*S*H. The only place I wanted to go was to my ballet class that was in Mansfield. Ballet was my passion and I took classes with little girls, since there was no adult class. I didn't seem to care as long as I was doing ballet. I didn't go anywhere else and didn't do anything; not even house work. Then one day, June, a teacher in the elementary school gave me a book called *A Walk Across America*. I started coming out of my depression while reading the book; out of the darkness and into the light.

I still felt like I could do more with my life. I wanted to excel more than anybody else in my family. Of course, I could never surpass Arvids' brother, Robert with his three PhD's. If I earn a doctorate, then my family will hold me in higher regard and I will feel better about myself. When I enrolled at Penn State for the summer of 1986, I encountered sexual harassment from one of my professors. Then I visited Pittsburgh University and enrolled there for the school year 1986–1987. It impressed me that all over the campus signs read, "Sexual Harassment is Against the Law." I took a sabbatical from the school district and went to live in Pittsburgh for a year plus one summer session. I finished all my course work in that time and applied for my dissertation study. It was accepted and I went home to my teaching job. Females from grades three, five, and eight from the school district became my subjects. The district gave me time during the school day to go interview the girls who had returned their parental permission slips. This action from the superintendent started a dissent among the faculty in the district. I was given special privileges that the rest weren't getting.

My dissertation was titled *The Relationship of Mathematics Achievement to Expected Career Choice for Females in Grades Three, Five and Eight in a Rural School District*. I interviewed 108 girls and gave each of them a shiny new Kennedy half-dollar. It took a year to gather and interpret the data and write up the results. Then I went before my dissertation committee for final review and to defend my study. Everything was acceptable and I sent my dissertation to the bookbinding company. The dissertation proved to be a very difficult, arduous and time-consuming endeavor. For the last time, I walked to the podium to receive my third degree, a doctorate in education and curriculum. I felt a great sense of accomplishment, what no one else in my family or the school district had achieved. Even the superintendent did not have his PhD.

The next school year my colleagues at the elementary school started to treat me with an attitude. They called me Doc and asked me all kinds of questions as if I should know everything now that I have my PhD. I felt humiliated from the sarcasm, and for the first time, I thought the PhD was a big mistake. I was now alienated. I hung my head and tried to hide my PhD, as if it didn't exist. The superintendent had nothing in mind for me at the district level and so I grew very discontent.

That summer I drove to West Palm Beach, Florida to see my friend Ellen Roupp. While I was there, I filled out an application to teach in Palm Beach County; had some interviews; then I drove back home and started another year at Liberty Elementary. At the end of September, I got a call from the Palm Beach County School District to teach Reading at Wellington Landings Middle School. I gave my school district two weeks notice, packed my car with enough stuff to start housekeeping and drove back to Florida. Not missing a day, I reported for work on Monday, October 10, 1989 in Wellington.

It was very difficult at first; like being in another country except that English was spoken mostly. I went through some hard times, but persevered, because I was determined. I enrolled in ballet classes twice a week and this kept me sane. Getting involved in church activities helped me to unload my tractor-trailer full of emotional baggage. By 1992, I had made the decision to start working toward certification as principal and took Saturday classed at Nova University. Back to studying again! After four years in Florida, in 1994, I sold my house in Liberty and bought a new house in Wellington, a beautiful Spanish style home in an upscale community. It was a good decision. In 1998, I had an in-ground pool with a Jacuzzi installed. I thought life was now at its zenith.

Not so! In September, (1994), I got the shingles. In October, I came down with pneumonia; was in the hospital five days; and missed three weeks of school.

The illness weakened my body and recovery was very slow, taking more than a year to get my strength back. It was enough to keep the inside and outside of the house in good shape and work in school every day. I dropped the idea of finishing the certification for principal even though, I was only six credits from finishing. This concluded my formal education, and I never took classes for credit again.

I am now retired and living in Liberty again, in yet another new house. For all of my striving and degrees, I never felt successful in a capacity that I wanted to be employed. I guess that was my destiny!

Graduation from Liberty High School, 1958

August 23, 1975
Master of Education, Mansfield State College
Melanie, Laima, Baiba, Tim, Dean, Jim

14

Arvids

I cannot end my story without including this chapter about Arvids. By nature he was a very quiet man. He didn't leave Jew Hill very often, spending most of his time in the greenhouses. Making plants grow became his life. He would send mother to get whatever he needed for fixing or building. She did it willingly. He ordered all of his seeds from catalogs. The large things he needed, he had delivered like lumber, blocks or top soil. His life revolved around the greenhouses, but he also worked at the foundry every day, five days a week. He spent mornings in the greenhouses and evenings at the foundry. In his later years, after retiring from the foundry, he became almost a recluse. The only time he left Jew Hill was to have his hair cut. Mother did everything else.

At the foundry he cleaned the machines where pipefittings were made, shoveling the shavings into a wheelbarrow and then wheeling the load outside to dump in a pile. He did this for thirty-five years. He was offered a machine job several times, but declined every time because he liked what he was doing. He remarked that he was the only one who could go outside many times a day and get a breath of fresh air. The rest of the workers had to stay by their machines all day. He was happy to be taking the wheelbarrow for a walk.

If his life was making plants grow, then Mother was the love of his life. He loved her with abandon. He handed over all of his money to her every week. She was the banker, the accountant, and the jewel in his eyes. They loved each other with tenderness.

Mother never worked outside the home again from the time when we left Latvia, but she worked tirelessly by Arvids' side in the greenhouses. When the spring planting season was over, mother wanted to travel. All she needed was a driver and she would provide the rest. I got to travel with her to many places, as I was the designated driver. Twice I accompanied her on the Amtrak to go out west.

By the end of June, Arvids started the geranium cuttings, poinsettia cuttings and Easter Lilies. They needed his ever-watchful eye so they didn't get too much sun, or dry out. Nobody could do this job for him. He had to stay with his beloved plants or there would not be flowers for the appropriate times. He knew when to open the windows and when to put a shade cover on or take it off. I don't know how he did it, but the poinsettias always bloomed right around Christmas and the Easter Lilies opened up just a week before Easter.

As I look back at all the things he did, he had to be close to a multi-talented genius. He built four greenhouses, stick by stick and glass pane by glass pane with Maris' help for the first one. The fourth greenhouse never got the glass panes but was covered with durable plastic. First and foremost, he was a horticulturist. He was also an incredible carpenter. What he designed on paper, he could build out of lumber. When he built things, they lasted a lifetime. He designed the heating system in the greenhouses that was comparable to heating engineers and then installed it. He was a bricklayer and understood electrical systems very well.

In the winter the greenhouse heating was crucial. He devised two back-ups for everything that had to do with the heating system. The big boiler was the primary source of heat. At first he used slab wood, and then changed the grates to burn coal. All of this required Arvids to constantly monitor the boiler. Then he had the boiler converted to natural gas and it made heating the greenhouses much easier but at a much higher cost.

Should the power go off, which it did often in the winter, he had an alarm rigged-up to go off in his bedroom. A large thermometer hung in the main greenhouse. This thermometer was hooked to a set of flashlight batteries that were wired to his bedroom. When the power went off or if the heat in the main greenhouse got down to forty degrees, the alarm would go off. He would then start the generator to run the circulator. The generator had a back up gas-powered pump in case the generator didn't start. The greenhouses each had a wood-fired stove. The main greenhouse had a firebrick furnace that he designed and built. It was constructed under the middle rack and was almost as long as the entire length of the greenhouse. He fired up this furnace with slab wood and the bricks radiated heat for a long time. All of this was just for the "blooming" of the poinsettias and lilies at the right time and to ensure that the geraniums would winter over.

This was the life he led and liked. He never made big money because he sold his plants and flowers too reasonably. The plants and flowers were always of very high quality. In the spring, people descended upon Jew Hill like flocks of geese and carried out plants and flowers along with the soil in wooden flats made by

Maris, and also plastic one dozen packs. I often wonder how many tons of soil actually walked off from the hill.

Arvids liked my flair for planting cemetery pots. Once he showed me how to do one, I was on cemetery pot duty every year. This gave me a chance to be creative and so I enjoyed it. In return I could have all of the flower and vegetable plants I wanted or needed. And every year, I planted lots and lots of flowers.

I really didn't get to know Arvids. He seemed to put a wall up between us. I thought it was because he didn't like me. After all, I wasn't his daughter and Maris being the only boy, wasn't his son. I felt we were not too important to him. He never put as much in words as he did in his actions. I was denied the real love I needed from a father figure. For Maris it was worse, because he used to get the belt when he did something not to Arvids' liking.

In the fall of 1988, Arvids started complaining about pain in his left shoulder and right knee. When I came over in the evening to visit them, Arvids was visibly in pain. I pulled mother in the kitchen and tried to convince her to take him to the doctor.

"He won't go," she simply replied.

"But it could be something serious," I pushed on.

"He doesn't want me to make an appointment, and that is that."

Several weeks later, I again tried to convince her that he should go to the doctor. By now, I think they are both in denial. She finally made an appointment, but he convinced her to cancel it. I tried over and over to get him to the doctor, but to avail. Sometime in April, he finally agreed to see a doctor. He was diagnosed with bone cancer.

Mother was very upset about the news of the cancer and said to me, "Why didn't you tell me you thought it might be cancer last fall?"

"I am not a doctor and can't make that kind of a statement," I replied.

Arvids was admitted to the Williamsport Hospital for diagnosis and observation. The hospital sent him home with medications by the dozen. The pharmacy was supposed to have all of the prescriptions filled by the time we got there, so Arvids wouldn't have to wait in the car too long. The wait turned out to be more than an hour and I was livid!

When we got to mother's house, I drove the car right up to the front door so he wouldn't have to try to go up the steps into the kitchen. Mother and I tried to help him out of the car and on to the porch. We couldn't hold him and he went down between the porch and the car.

"My legs won't work," said Arvids.

"I'm going in to call Donny Wheeland, maybe he can bring one of his boys to help us get him inside," I suggested to mother.

"No, no don't call anybody, we will get him in somehow," she protested. I took matters into my own hands and called Donny against her wishes. In a few minutes, Donny and his son, Ray, were at our front door. They carried him in and put him in his reclining chair. It was very obvious that Arvids could not walk. Then I called his doctor, and related the story to him. The doctor said to bring him back to the hospital. I called for the ambulance and followed it down to the Williamsport Hospital. The doctor met us in the emergency room. The doctor told Arvids to tell him when he feels the pin jab on his back. The doctor started to prick the skin at the lower back. No response. Again he pricked the skin; again, no response. For a few minutes the doctor thought that maybe Arvids didn't understand that he is tell him when he feels the pin. Finally, the doctor pricked the pin near his shoulder blades and Arvids said he could feel the pin. The expression on the doctor's face changed drastically. The seriousness I saw on the doctor's face, told me the news would not be good. He was paralyzed from his waist down! Arvids' was admitted again. The whole family was at the hospital. Maris flew in from the west coast.

Then Arvids took a turn for the worse. He was placed in the intensive care unit and had a tube put in his mouth. He tried desperately to remove the tube. His hands were tied down so couldn't work at the tube. Somehow that man worked at it until he got that tube out of his throat! When I called the nurse in, she said we wouldn't put it back in and just let him rest. He was bleeding from the rectum as I saw the crisp white sheet ooze a bright red color along his sides. Mother asked me to stay with Arvids that night. He was not expected to live through the night. I agreed. I prayed then, dozed in my chair by bits and checked on him every so often. He seemed to be resting. By morning, he was awake and asking about Mother, where she was. When is she coming? When the doctors came in, he had stopped bleeding and was awake and aware. Not only had he made it through the night, but also his condition had improved. He was soon moved to a private room upstairs. I got on the phone and anxiously called Mother about the good news.

Mother was so overjoyed to hear the news and gave me all the credit for his survival through the night.

"I am eternally grateful to you for saving his life," she declared.

I said, "I really didn't do anything." She insisted that my being there helped him to improve. When Mother got to the hospital, she was all smiles and gladness. I was enjoying all the attention and suddenly felt important.

He was kept in the hospital a few more days for observation. Again, I was asked to stay with him all night. He didn't like staying alone and nobody else was available. When everyone had left the hospital, Arvids told me to bring my chair over and sit next to him, that he wanted to talk to me. This is the occasion he chose to tell me that he had always loved me, but he just never told me.

"Can you ever forgive me?" he asked.

"Yes I forgive you for that," I replied.

Then he started to weep.

"You are a very good person, intelligent, ambitious. You work hard. You have earned a Ph.D. And you can find beauty and truth wherever you go," came the words from his mouth. By now I was also crying. We talked on about life and what is important. And for the first time in my life I knew whom Arvids really was—a deep thinking person, full of wisdom, ability and kindness, capable of love. Oh, I wish we could have talked like this forty some years ago! I might have had a better concept of myself. But now on his deathbed, he is pouring his heart out to me. I am a better person because of his outpouring.

"Will you give me a kiss on the cheek? I will know you have forgiven me for sure then. I am so sorry for how I have treated you," was the surprising request.

"Sure, I can forgive you. I can forgive anyone who asks," I replied and bent down and kissed him on the cheek.

He immediately wept with tears flooding his cheeks. Then I gave him a hug. The rest of the night, he was very restless, calling out about every fifteen minutes to give him a drink; to fluff his pillows; to cover his feet; and to uncover his feet. I left for home at seven in the morning, changed my clothes and went to my teaching job at Liberty Elementary School.

When Arvids was sent home, mother had a hospital bed ready for him and he was put on Hospice. I don't think mother knew what Hospice meant. She just understood that she was going to get help taking care of him at home. The Hospice nurse came about three times a week and then she spent most of her time on paperwork at the kitchen table. That left me to tend to Arvids' many needs. I went to Mother's every night after school and cleaned his triple lumen, exercised his legs and arms and talked. While Maris was home, he helped with Arvids' care. That relieved me for a few days.

In June the pain got too much for him, mother moved him to a hospital near his daughter's home in Valley Forge. She had beckoned mother to bring him down there and just maybe they could help him get better. From then on mother went into deep and complete denial about his death. He was not going to die and that was it!

He stayed in a state of stupor. But he could hear and understand everything we would say. His neck and arms were swelled up. He was no longer getting intravenus, and I hoped mother did not notice. If she did, she never said anything about it. He opened his eyes every so often and looked around.

"Just don't bury me alive," he announced and went back into his sleep. I was with him day and night so mother could go get some rest. During the day she stayed by his side so I could get some sleep.

On August 3, 1989, with just mother and me in the room, Arvids took a big gasping breath and his soul passed into Heaven. "What just happened here?" Mother asked.

"Mrs. Kalnins, Arvids has passed away, we cannot do any more for him," said one of the doctors.

"No, there must be some mistake," she protested.

The doctor stood there with her but didn't say anything more. He waited until it started to sink in of what had just happened.

Mother then went to Arvids' bedside to say goodbye to him. I was speechless and couldn't find the words to say to her. I left the room to do what I had to do.

God saw you getting tired
And a cure was not to be.
So he put his arms around you
And whispered "Come to Me."
With tearful eyes we watched you,
And saw you pass away.
Although we loved you dearly,
We could not make you stay.
A golden heart stopped beating,
Hardworking hands at rest.
God broke our hearts to prove to us,
He only takes the best. *

*Used by permission from *Life Celebration*

I made some phone calls while mother stayed with the body, holding his chin up with her hand so his mouth would be closed in death. She talked to him and stroked his face and told him over and over, "Teti, don't leave me, please don't leave me. I cannot go on without you. Please don't go!"

This kind of love I had never witnessed before. She stayed with the body for an hour just talking to him and stroking his face, kissing his cheeks. The doctors let her stay with the body for as long as she wanted.

The next day arrangements were made to bring the body back to Liberty for the funeral. I then began the two hundred miles back to Liberty. It was a most difficult trip. She was stressing out big time. Her conversation turned bitter and the meltdown started with every statement to bring me down too. I felt like I was under attack, like I was Pearl Harbor! Emotionally, I was a wreck! I couldn't take it anymore and started to sob. Mother was relentless. I knew she needed to vent to someone, but I was exhausted too. I know she wanted me to cry, to hurt as much as she did. But my main concern was getting us back to Liberty safely.

I had just missed the exit to get off the turnpike and we had to go much farther north to get to the next exit. I spotted a place on the turnpike where I could pull off and then stopped the car.

"I can't drive and listen to this discourse directed at me. I have to concentrate and focus on the road. I don't want to be driving in this heavy traffic when I am this upset. So, please consider me for right now, otherwise we are not going to get home," I finally said assertively.

She apologized to me and we rode home in a much better state of mind. I stayed with mother that night and slept on the couch. Maris flew in from the west coast again as we prepared for the funeral.

Mother held up very well under all the duress. The open casket viewing, and the funeral were held in the Liberty Lutheran Church. The church filled up with people who came to pay their respects to a man who had cultivated such wonderful plants for all of these years. Reverend Klinger was retired and living in the Liberty area again. Mother called on him to deliver the eulogizing message.

As we filed out of the church, I placed a single yellow long stemmed rose on Arvids' chest and said, "Goodbye Teti."

After the funeral, Mother would not set foot in the Liberty Church again; instead, she attended church at Friedens. Mother went down hill after she lost her beloved Arvids. In December of 1992 she was diagnosed with enlarged Thymus gland at Divine Providence Hospital. This condition was making it difficult for her to swallow. The diagnosis was followed with an operation to remove the thymus. The doctors could not get it all since it was too close to the main artery. She had radiation from December through April. Maris returned to Liberty in April and was there to keep the greenhouses going.

Mother was OK for a while, and went into remission for four years. She continued to work with plants in the greenhouses. Then the cancer returned as Lymphoma. The doctors gave her what they called a miracle drug (prednisone) from Italy. It helped for about three months. She died of complications of thymus cancer in October of 1997. The love story and life of Laima and Arvids has come to an end. Selah.

Arvids and Laima

15

Return to Latvia

On June 25, 1990 began a journey that I could only dream about. Forty-six years ago, I had left my homeland with my family and sailed away on the Baltic Sea for worlds unknown amidst a terrible war. And now I will return to my homeland, again by sailing on the Baltic Sea, but this time under much different circumstances.

Standing in my driveway Mother and I hugged each other and both of us broke into tears. In that moment I understood how much this trip meant to her, and I believe she wished she could go too. She has been preparing for this trip for weeks; drawing maps, writing directions, jotting down names and addresses for finding people and places. She was mainly concerned that I find her parents' graves and take pictures.

As I pulled out of Liberty Lane (my home on Jew Hill) at 4:30 PM, I was filled with excitement and with tears flowing down my cheeks. I looked back and saw Mother still standing in my driveway waving her arm. She was probably crying too. It was a very emotional moment and a memorable one. I arrived at my half-sister's house at 8:30 PM. We opened a bottle of champagne and made a toast to Latvia.

And thus the journey began with excitement and much anticipation. The small refugee girl, afraid of everything, has grown up now and become a world traveler! I had overcome my greatest fear of all, flying. Although it was not my first time to fly, but it was the first time I was flying over the ocean. My traveling partner, Janis and I along with the rest of the Latvian party arrived at JFK Airport at 4:00 PM. amidst heavy and congested traffic. The international part of JFK looked like a vast airplane farm. The airplanes were lined up around the perimeter of the airport and looked like cattle that had come in for a feeding and milking. There are planes here from almost every country in the world. Duty free shops are everywhere with prices much bigger than my pocketbook.

We boarded the Air France jumbo jet about 6:30 PM but didn't take off until it was close to eight o'clock. It must take a long time to board 350 passengers. The date was now June 26. The airplane was so humongous that you think you are in a large convention hall. There are two levels of passengers and six bathrooms every 20 seats. I was really surprised at myself about how little fear I had on take-off, unlike my maiden voyage across the states to San Diego to see my Marine son. My excitement built as I thought about "Paree," the first leg of the journey to my homeland. I was so nervous then that I couldn't eat my meal. On this night, however, I ate heartily: salmon appetizer, filet mignon, vegies, salad, roll, cake and champagne. Everything the stewardesses brought us was complementary including the New York Times, drinks, headphones, pillow and blanket. The monitors were showing a movie and every so often revealed the plane's progress across the ocean. I tried to sleep but it was next to impossible.

The monitor showed that we were very near Paris and it was seven o'clock AM in France. After breakfast, we prepared to land. I could not understand anything they were announcing on the loudspeakers even though they supposedly translated all information into English. I think the French accent made it difficult to understand. Looking out the window I could see nothing but the white fluffy stuff.

"I hope we are soon out of the clouds so I can see Paris from the air," I told Janis.

"Ja," is all he said.

Suddenly, a very loud crunching, crashing sound sends me up the panic tree! This is it; I'm dead! My heart had jumped out but my sight was still in place. Nobody else seemed to be in a panic. I looked out the window and still saw the white fluffy stuff but on closer inspection I saw the yellow lines of the tarmac racing by extremely fast. "The eagle had landed!" I breathed a sigh of relief.

Inside the terminal it was as confusing as the fog outside. Janis is totally befuddled and is getting grumpy. We are told to go to the passport checkpoint area. But c how can we get over there? Everything is closed off with glass walls. I felt like a mouse in a maze trying to get to the cheese. I scouted around, much to Janis' disgust, until I found the information desk. If I had listened to him, we would still be sitting in The de Gaulle Airport terminal. The young lady at the desk told me in broken English to "go by the customs" and I can get out that way. I summoned Janis and we went **by** the customs but it led us to nowhere.

Then I figured out that we had to go **through** the customs checkpoint and not **by** it! Just a little international misunderstanding, but it had cost us about an hour. Janis seemed to be totally helpless in any situation. I decided right then that

I would never travel with Janis again. Once I found the other side of the terminal and we had found the correct gate, I wanted to see about a bus tour of Paris. By now it was too late for the tour bus. Much to the protest of Janis, I hired a taxi to get a whirlwind tour of Paris. Janis would not go. He was worried that I would not get back in time for the connecting plane to Stockholm, six hours later. I went anyway.

Everybody in Paris seems to drive terribly fast. My taxi driver had unhooked his speedometer so I couldn't tell how fast he was going. The streets are just as congested as I saw in New York City. Besides cars, the congestion includes motorcyclists, bicyclists and pedestrians. All of the above take chances and zip in and out of traffic. I witnessed an accident where a motorcyclist tried to squeeze between two cars ahead of us. The driver on the left squeezed him too close and he ended up laying the motorcycle down right in front of us. My driver was able to stop, but then pulled right around the accident, as did everybody else. The cyclist seemed to be pinned under his motorcycle. As we drove off, I could hear the three men start to shout at each other. It probably did not take long for the police to get there because they seem to be everywhere. All of the policemen looked to be no more than seventeen or eighteen years old.

The driver only spoke French and Korean and I only spoke Latvian and English. Somehow he understood that I wanted a quick tour of Paris and he took me to the three main points of interest: Notre Dame Cathedral, The Eiffel Tower, and The Arch of Triumph. The cobblestone streets in Paris are narrow, quaint, and very busy. In two hours the tour was over. Although communicating was not easy, the driver was very clear about how much I owed him.

"Hoondred dollah!" he announced.

"What?" I asked.

"Hoondred dollah," he repeated.

"No, too much!" I protested.

"Ja, hoondred dollah," he reiterated.

I reluctantly gave him a hundred dollar bill and got out of the car giving him an angry look. It cost me plenty, but I had seen Paris! Janis was glad to see me back in plenty of time for boarding the plane for our next leg of the journey. Six hours have passed since we first arrived at The de Gaulle Airport.

Hot, sweaty, tired and thirsty we boarded Air France for Stockholm, Sweden. This is a smaller plane than the one that brought us across the ocean. The plane is delayed for forty-five minutes because of a bad storm, and I feel very nervous about this flight. Once we were in the air, the flight only took two hours.

After landing, we stood in a long line to get through passport check, but once we were through, Janis summoned a limo, and we were on our way to the Central Hotel in Stockholm. The room we have at the hotel is small but very clean.

When this trip was in the planning stages, I told Janis, "I want to sleep alone, so make sure there are two beds in the hotel room or you will be sleeping on the floor." It had two single beds. Yes!

Janis ordered a pizza and after showers we were ready for some shuteye. Before going to sleep, I called Mother to tell her that we were safely in Stockholm and she told me the exciting news, that Melanie has a baby boy. She named him Dean, much to my chagrin. Mother tells me that both, the new mother and baby are doing fine. I went to sleep quickly but at 3:00 AM, no more sleep. It was already daylight outside. I'm not used to summer solstice and darkness only three or four hours per night.

June 28. I had just dozed off again when Janis awakened me to go eat breakfast. A Swedish continental breakfast is very much like American hotels offer. However, the cold dry cereal in Sweden is served with plain yogurt instead of milk, so I chose the pastries instead.

In the afternoon, I ventured out on my own to do some sight seeing. I went inside of a church with the doors wide open, and sat down to pray. I asked God for his blessings on the rest of the journey and gave thanks for this wonderful journey back to my original home. Our boat, *The Happy Ship*, From Baltic Star Lines, would not be here until June thirtieth. Since it was a rainy day, I slept or watched TV until it was time to go to bed.

June 29, Janis and I took a tour bus and a boat ride to sightsee Stockholm. It truly is a beautiful city, with its ancient stone buildings skillfully preserved. The city is very clean and flowers are blooming everywhere. I did not see any trash on any of the streets. The tour guide was multi lingual and translated everything into four languages; German, French, Swedish and English.

Later in the day I went for a walk and found a supermarket. I bought food for our supper and some beer for Janis.

June 30. I was packed and ready to go by 9:00 AM. After breakfast, Janis got a taxi to take us to the dock. We had to wait there all day, since *The Happy Ship* would not dock until 7:00 PM. The situation reminded me of the war days; waiting with our belongings. The docking pier was in old town Stockholm. Since it was going to be a long wait I decided to walk to old town to do more sight seeing. Janis again was not pleased with my wandering. His fear was that I might not get back in time to board the boat. I went anyway.

The old town of Stockholm was like walking back into history; ancient and quaint, like medieval times. Every street was filled with unique novelty shops. Street musicians were on every corner. The streets were still cobblestone, but very narrow, the sidewalks even narrower. The place was filled with throngs of people walking and enjoying everything like I was. No motor vehicles were allowed on these ancient streets. Nothing can compare to what I long to see in Latvia.

I returned from my tour of old town of Stockholm in time to get in line for our boarding tickets. It was still a couple hours wait to board. Then Janis put up a fuss when I said I was getting in line for our boarding and meal tickets. He said he doesn't need any. He seems to be totally oblivious and in a world of his own. I know he doesn't hear well but when he does hear, he doesn't seem to understand. I am frustrated but then I feel sorry for him too; he has a good heart.

Then I saw it. The Baltic Star appeared in the distance. Suddenly, I became very emotional. I shed a tear or two and then snapped some pictures. This is the ship that would make a historic journey into Latvia and I was part of it! We boarded by 7:15 and watched the ship pull away from the dock while two Latvian flags were being raised. We found our cabin to be very small but clean and satisfactory. It was equipped with bunk beds, our own private bathroom and a porthole. This is a lot better than what most people had for accommodations.

The evening meal was served by 8:30 PM. The spread was elaborate with a hot and cold bar. Every party was assigned to a certain table in one of the two dining rooms for the duration of the trip, which took just overnight. After the meal, Janis was very tired and went right to bed taking the top bunk. I looked around the ship and found two cocktail lounges. I had a couple of drinks; then I went out on the deck and sat enjoying the evening fade away. The sunset at ten o'clock was a sight to behold over the horizon of the endless sea.

By 11:00 PM the ship was finally on the Baltic Sea and it still wasn't dark outside. When the wind began to gust, I went to the cabin and slipped into bed by 1:00AM. The ship seemed to be moving at a pretty good clip as I fell asleep.

At 3:00 AM it was daylight again. It is hard to get used to these daylight hours. After lunch, we were informed that we would be in Riga at 3:15 PM. When *The Happy Ship* passed into The Gulf of Riga, I took both cameras with me and went down to the sun deck to take my place along the railing. But people had already lined the railing so I had to stand behind them and videotape between two other people. Soon the ship was sailing up the Daugava River. The first sign of life on the river was a sailboat with the Latvian flag. As the ship made its way, I got my first glimpse of what the country looked like. Along the Eastern side of the river all that was mainly visible were old rusty, algae covered war ships and some cranes that were used to load the ships. There they sat wasting away by the shores. Just one crane was moving along the entire river. Everything looks gray and dingy, virtually a wasteland. A few people here and there are sitting on a very narrow beach. No one is in the water, maybe because it is the color of very strong iced tea. Some people are fishing and some people wave at us.

As we got closer to the Port of Riga, my excitement mounted. My first dim view of Latvia had not dampened my spirit. A pilot in a small boat met us and guided us into the harbor. But before the ship was allowed to dock, our tour director made an announcement.

"In order to dock, the ship has to fly the Soviet flag at the highest point. We have a choice however, we can fly the red flag or we can turn around and go back to Stockholm."

Everyone agreed to fly the red flag with the hammer and cycle. There was talk among the tourists that we could wrap the Red flag around the pole and tape it. We all snickered at the idea of it. As we approached the dock, sixteen Latvian flags were waving abundantly in the wind. At the highest point of the ship was the red flag. Like a miracle, everyone watched as the wind wrapped the red flag around the pole and kept it there tight. We all giggled at this sight. God's intervention was awesome! I bought some bananas just before getting off the ship, as did most other people. The tour group later became known as "The Baltic Bible Banana Boat." You see people in Latvia had not seen a banana since before WWII, and were not allowed to own a Bible. So we brought both things in for the first time. I love this *parastroika*!

On the shore were multitudes of Latvians, kept back by a barricade. As the ship was docking, all of us on the ship began singing Latvian hymns. The Latvians on the ground joined us. What a beautiful chorus! Tears rolled down my cheeks as I cherished this breathtaking moment. Little did I know there would be a lot more surprises for me? Then a band, dressed in Soviet army garb played a Russian marching song. *The Happy Ship* had made a historical journey, being the first foreign ship with all Latvian passengers aboard to come into the Riga Port. And I was part of it!

On the pavement in front of the ship, two Soviet soldiers were marching back and forth to make sure nobody tried to get on the ship. Before we debarked, all of the people on the ground were told to go inside the port. At checkpoint, Russian soldiers took our American passport and gave us a Russian passport. *The Happy Ship* became our hotel and we had to return to the ship every night. At night we got our own passport back and every morning we had to give it to the controllers. Later this trip was nicknamed The Baltic Banana Bible Boat because we brought

Bibles and bananas to Latvia. Bananas had not been seen in Latvia for fifty years and Bibles were forbidden.

After the passport check, I started to walk through the crowd that had left a narrow path for the visitors to pass through. I walked on through the crowd looking for Mudeet not knowing if she even got my message of my arrival today.

"That must be her," a voice on my left spoke. "Baibin?"

"Mudeet!" I exclaimed.

"Ja!"

I threw my arms around her and kissed her cheek while the flood of tears flowed uncontrollably down my face. She presented me with a pretty bouquet of flowers, as is the Latvian custom. Alfreds, an uncle of Mudeet, whom I had met when he came to the states a year ago, accompanied her to the port. I greeted him with a kiss on the cheek. Alfreds is an uncle to my father too. I had tried to reach him by phone all day the day before I left, but did not reach him. I tried once more at midnight and to my surprise I got through. I asked him if he could get a message to Mudeet that I would be in Port of Riga on July 1st. I was so happy that she had received the message.

Alfreds went to get a taxi while Mudeet talked in a soft voice about how bad things really were in Latvia. Whenever somebody walked by, she lowered her voice to a whisper or stopped talking completely. The taxi took us to Alfred's apartment in Riga. Alfreds tried to give the driver rubles for the fare but he said he wanted American dollars and turned his head toward me. The smallest bill I had was a ten, so I gave it to the driver. Then I saw Mudeet's mouth drop to the floor and her eyes were as big as the moon. She later exclaimed how that was way too much to give the driver, but for that same money he said he would take us back to the port and take the two of them back to Alfred's apartment.

My first look at a city apartment in Riga is appalling. The outside is overgrown with weeds, probably never gets mowed. It is very slummy looking. The stairway is dingy, dark and dirty. The building is five stories high and Alfreds lives on the fifth floor. No elevator either. As we are climbing the stairs, Mudeet tells me that her mother died on March 18, 1989, and that her mother had remembered my birthday was that day. This statement moved me to tears that my aunt would remember my birthday on her deathbed. I felt like I was very special at that moment. And that was only the beginning.

The apartment inside was also a little dingy and dated of about fifty years ago. The flooring is painted over worn linoleum. Two small rooms made up the apartment. The living room triples as a bedroom with a fold out couch, and a dining area. In the corner of this so-called living room is a small box of what seems to be their three-year-old grandson's toys. Toys are ordinary things like a tuna fish can, some lids, a stick, some string and other tin cans. The boy lives with the grandparents so both parents can work. This is very common in Latvia. The grandparents often raise the children so the parents can eke out a living in another town. Alfred's wife yells at the little boy all the time. One time she even threatened him with the belt. Poor little "fella" was expected to play only with his makeshift toys all day long.

The kitchen is the size of a double bed and is equipped with a small refrigerator under the counter, an apartment sized gas stove, a little sink, and one cupboard. There is room for only one person at a time in the kitchen. Since it is summer, there is no hot water. The heating source is shut off from April to November. When they need hot water, it is heated on the little apartment size gas stove. Another tiny room has a claw foot tub and a very small sink. The flushing toilet is in yet another small cubicle just big enough to hold a commode.

Alfreds' wife cooked some dinner, not too elaborate and we sat on the couch (also known as the dining room), and ate our meal.

After that the taxi driver took Alfreds, Mudeet and me back to the ship. I quickly changed into my Latvian folk costume, *Zemgale*, the name derived from the area of my birth. Then we got into line to march 2 x 2 to the Doma Lutheran Cathedral, for the liturgical "high mass." The stone cathedral is clean and bright and beautiful inside. It is a huge structure, with very high ceilings and a pipe organ in the back balcony where the angelic voices of the choir also sit. When the organist played the huge organ, the sound went right through my body and touched my soul. Nearly 2000 people filled the church. Communion was served to those who were members or had been members of the church. I did not go up since I had never set foot in this cathedral before today. The service was very long but meaningful.

I was overcome with emotion. Here I am in the country of my birth; sitting in this gorgeous church; listening to the beautiful music; wearing my native costume; holding a pretty bouquet of colorful flowers; and my long lost cousin sitting beside me. I was in awe of it all. Overwhelmed with this entire setting, I felt like I was living in a dream. It seemed surreal. Not even the hot, sticky weather fazed me. I gave a prayer thanking God for all of his blessings. Little did I know that tomorrow there would be even bigger and better surprises.

Mudeet took a taxi back to Alfred's house, and I walked back to my floating hotel with a group of other Latvians. We walked along the Daugava River. For a small distance, there was a concrete walk along the highway, but it ended abruptly and we all had to walk in the grass. Now it seems pretty sure that nowhere, absolutely nowhere, does the grass get mowed. During the entire walk back, I smelled sewer. The stench was so bad that I held my hand over my mouth and nose, sickening. Then I surmised what probably happened is that they dump human waste sewers in the river at night, so it didn't smell in the daytime.

I am concerned about Mudeet. She appears to be very somber. Her face is so stern that a smile was not possible and her hands shook continuously. I felt sorry for her and wanted to help. She must have had a very hard life, I decided.

Back in my room, I noticed that both of Janis' suitcases were gone and on my bed were a dozen red roses. The note said, "I will be back in three days." I was quite relieved that Janis didn't expect me spend any time with him. I wanted to spend as much time with my family as I possibly could.

The night was very hot and sticky. I went out on the dock to get cooled off and had a conversation with one of the sailor on our ship. The ever present Soviet guards paced back and forth in front of the ship to make sure nobody tried escape from Latvia. The sailor explained that once a person is on the ship, he/she is on foreign soil and therefore free. As we talked the two guards kept pacing closer and closer to us as they passed. I think they wanted to hear what we were talking about. The ship was guarded "twenty-four-seven" like it was The Tomb of the Unknown Soldier in Arlington.

July 2. I put on my Liz Claiborne dress and took one of my suitcases with me to give to Mudeet. It was filled with over-the-counter medications, toiletries, clothing and coffee, etc. The woman at the customs check stopped me and asked if I had some gifts in my suitcase and I said, "Yes." Then she wanted to know what kind of gifts and I told her, at which time I thought she would take the suitcase away from me. But much to my relief, she let me go through, suitcase and all.

I met Mudeet in the station and we went out on the street until she decided what we would do today. Then she went to the telephone booth and tried to call Oyars, her brother. When she finally got through to his work number, she said he was coming right over. His office was in the tallest, most modern building in Riga. In the meanwhile, it had started to rain. At a distance we saw a man walking with an umbrella.

"That is him walking toward us now," Mudeet said.

"That's Oyars!" I exclaimed.

Tall, dark, and handsome; he was slim; dressed in shirt and tie. The most gorgeous man I have ever seen. And he is my cousin! He has so much charisma! He greeted me warmly and smiled as he welcomed me to my homeland. I can see that his life was a lot different from hers, even though they both have engineering degrees. I can see that something is wrong between brother and sister. Right away I think it is because I have inconvenienced both of them. I would find out the real reason later.

"How could you do this?" Oyars spoke to his sister.

"I don't want to be in your way; I will just walk around Riga myself to see the sights," I offered.

"No," Oyars protested, "I won't let you do that."

In a few minutes he had reached his son at work and Ainars came over with his company car. After giving Mudeet the suitcase full of daily necessities, we picked up Oyars' wife, Velta at her work place. Ainars then took us to Oyars' house where his wife Velta prepared dinner for us. We ate on the living room coffee table as the kitchen table was not much bigger than a postage stamp (exaggeration) and could seat only two people. Later that afternoon we walked Mudeet to the train station to go back to her home in Kuldiga. It was a four-our ride for her to get home. Then Oyars told me the real reason he was so upset. Mudeet had not called him to let him know that I was coming and did not let him know that I had arrived until today. You have traveled halfway around the world and she brings you out in the street not knowing what to do next. After the explanation, I felt better. I had found two of my long lost cousins.

July 3. Today was set aside for meeting with Arvids' cousin, Biruta Urpens. Her son was coming to pick me up at the port station. I sat on a bench at the port with my name on a sign. Neither one of us knew each other. After we introduced each other, he drove back to his parents' home in Jurmala. The city is on the beach of the Gulf of Riga and is just north of Riga. I was amazed at the resemblance Biruta has to Arvids. Her eyes, nose, mouth, chin and her smile remind me very much of Arvids. They are cousins on his mother's side.

Their house, an old two-story farmhouse is immaculately kept. Flowerbeds are everywhere. A vegetable garden totally lacks of any weeds but has beautiful plants. A greenhouse is full of roses that they sell for some extra income. I am really impressed and even the grass is cut! At one time they owned many acres on this farm but now only have one-half of an acre. They were fortunate to be able to keep the house and they use it like we do here for a "bed and breakfast" type inn. Jurmala is known as a gulf resort. There is no indoor plumbing but their toilet is under the same roof as the rest of the house. Actually it is an outhouse but it is inside. There is no odor and the room is freshly painted. The kitchen however is in a separate shed from the house and the shower is in the boiler room, another shed. Everything is impeccably clean.

While I was at Biruta's home, she had other guests. One was from Germany and one was from Australia. Biruta put on a beautiful spread of food, a custom in every Latvian home, served on her dining room table graced with a beautiful lace tablecloth.

After the meal we went for a walk to the beach. When we got on the sand, I took off my shoes and set my feet in the Baltic Sea for the first time in my life. The water was cold and not many people were on the beach; some were actually in the water. The water was a dark, dirty and brown. The Soviet regime in Latvia had destroyed all of the waterways by dumping, who knows what, in the rivers and in the gulf. On my way back to the ship I asked Biruta's son to stop at an artist's house so I could buy a truly Latvian painting. I chose one with white birch trees and a small stream.

When I got back to the station, Oyars and Ainars were already waiting to take me on a tour of Riga. Our first stop was the freedom monument where I laid a bouquet of flowers as many other people had done. Then we walked around Old Riga that dates back many centuries. The old castle is still in tact and is used as the president's mansion. It is very much like Old Towne Stockholm, but dark, dreary and dirty.

"There is so much potential here for tourism," I thought, "If capitalism was only allowed."

Everywhere we went was the ever presence of the "Ruskie" soldiers. In Old Riga, a couple of these soldiers barged out of a building and were on the run heading toward us. I panicked again thinking they were going to arrest me or take my video camera or both. Oyars said not to worry. They sprinted right by us and were gone, much to my relief.

When I got back to the ship I found it difficult to sleep with all of the excitement of the day, my mind was still going strong. The last time I looked at my watch, it said 2 o'clock.

July 4. It was Independence Day, in the good old USA. Happy Birthday America! I am thinking about you. Today is the day I will go to my hometown, Bauska. After about a forty-five minute ride, our first stop was Rupniecibas Street, house # 13. As Oyars and I walked down the street, he asked me if I remember where the house is located.

"No."

"You are looking at it right now," Oyars said.

I **did** recognize it, but only after Oyars had pointed it out. I was looking at a sad looking structure. The only visible improvement in fifty years was a faded coat of Soviet green paint. It seemed like the only color Soviets made was that ugly green, except for a little red. The cobblestones on the street were broken up or missing. There were patches of macadam among the cobblestones and some places just plain mud. Water was running down the street from an unknown source. The whole street was dirty, gray and a mess. My window was still there but there were no flowers. The sound that was once embedded in my ears was gone too.

We walked to the back yard and it was in shambles too. Overgrown with grass and weeds, there was no sign of human inhabitation, even though thirteen names were written on a sign as residents. Then I spied my grandfather's gazebo, still in tact but barely hanging together. The boards were rotting and gray from the weathering all these years. The old horse shed and carriage shed were also holding together but not by much. The old outhouse we used back then is still in use today. This is the place where I lived and it was so beautiful when I was a small child. Now tears came to my eyes as I gazed at this wretched place.

The next stop was the Reverend's house appropriately named Church Street. We went up a dark dingy stairway and knocked on the reverends door. From inside we heard, "Ja." When Oyars explained what we wanted, Reverend Zibergs opened the door. The room gave an ancient appearance; something like one would see in a Charles Dickens story. The antique furniture was in very good condition. The glass door bookshelves went from floor to ceiling and were filled with old, old books. The Reverend's large desk sits in front of a dim window and is covered with papers and books. An old upright piano is against the wall. Several vases of wilting flowers were the only adornment in the room. Then he asks us to sit down while Oyars explained that I do not have a baptismal certificate and would he be able to look for the book that it was written in. I don't have a birth certificate either, so I though it would help if I had some kind of a birth document.

The reverend was in his nineties and seemed like he was in another world. Oyars asked him if he understood what we were asking for and he said, "Ja." Then he disappeared behind another door. Soon he returned with a couple of very old register books. I started looking in the 1939 book in which all the names were written by hand in ink. I could not find it because they were written in order the baptisms took place and I don't have an exact date just a year.

I tried going down through the names just one more time and exclaimed, "There it is; there it is!" I was baptized on June 24, 1939, (three months old) the day all Latvians celebrate the official arrival of summer—John's Day. The reason I had overlooked it was because my name is listed as Livija Baiba Ozols. The Reverend said he could make us a copy right away. While he is typing on the ancient typewriter, I had found Maris' baptism register and he made us a copy of that too. Then the Reverend put the all-important seal on it and both certificates were now official. Oyars tried to give him some money but the Reverend flatly refused it. Then we asked if he could show us the church I used to attend while my parents were still living in Bauska.

Ainars drove the four of us down the street from the Reverend's residence. Then the Reverend took a large ancient black key, out of his pocket and put it in the keyhole of the enormous gothic style door painted an emerald green. It was the largest key I had ever seen, at least ten inches long. The big black hinges were certainly dated to the middle ages. The immense door creaked as he opened it. Inside the narthex were two huge piles of wood on each side of the door. Another door opened into the sanctuary. Tears filled my eyes once again, as I slowly walked toward the altar then dropped on my knees to give a prayer of thanksgiving. Again I am overcome with emotion of this awesome place that linked me to the Lutheran church. In the side walls toward the front of the church were two really large headstones that were incorporated into the walls. They were about the size of a king sized bed. One was a woman and one was a man. They must have been very important people. On the stairway up to the pulpit the year 1645 is written in large numbers. The reverend told us that it shows the year the church was built. The altar was covered with white lace paraments and bouquets of wild flowers were everywhere. The reverend explained that a funeral was scheduled in the afternoon.

I went to the back of the church and climbed the wooden stairs that led to the choir loft and the pipe organ. Mother had told me that her grandfather played this organ at one time. The choir seating was plain straight benches without backs on them. This is also where Mother sat for her Sunday School lessons. There is so much personal history here that I feel like I am walking on hallowed ground. The Reverend pointed to the left corner of the church ceiling and told us the corner had been hit with shrapnel but that was all the damage the church had received from the war. He then explained that the stained-glass windows were removed by the Soviet government and sold for ammunition! No one could do anything about it. The windows were eventually replaced with plain glass by townspeople.

The pews in the church are wooden benches with a high back. To be seated in any pew, a person needed to open a small door. The inside and the outside of the church are painted white. The roof is high and steep, and painted green to match the front door. The towering steeple contains a small bell. The church looks better than most homes people live in.

Oyars wanted to show me the greenhouses Arvids and his mother operated. They were just outside the town. The garden house, where we spent the last night before leaving Bauska, has collapsed, but some of the large frames of the stalwart greenhouses still stand like old soldiers who never die. Everything is overgrown with tall weeds and grasses.

Next, the three of us went on River Street to see the house, #3, where Rudy spent his childhood. The house is pathetic; looks like an abandoned building. Again it is completely overgrown with tall weeds and grass. It is so sad. The street is still a dirt road like it was fifty some years ago.

Then it was on to the cemetery. I pulled out Mother's hand drawn map and we started searching for the plot. We looked all over the cemetery but nowhere could we find a stone with the name Tetins on it. Oyars went to ask the man (guard) in the little office about record books for an exact location, but the man replied there are no books. They were either destroyed or are in the archives in Moscow. The picture that Mother had given me had four concrete posts about two feet tall with a heavy chain fastened from post to post around the plot. The spot where Mother had designated that her parents' graves would be, there was a new stone with a Russian name on it. It was a recent grave as the death date was in January of 1990, and then I noticed one of the posts and the chain hanging from it, now on the ground. One of two things probably happened here: the Russian was buried on top of them or Mother's parents' bodies were dug up and discarded. Either one is a dreadful, wretched thought. I wasn't sure how I would break the news to Mother when I got back home. I told myself that I wouldn't say anything unless she asks. When she did ask, I told her what I had found.

She said, "No, that can't be. You must have made a mistake." Then she went in the other room and she never brought the subject up again. I think she was in denial. End of story. Selah.

The Ozols graves were amazingly in good shape, and under a huge oak tree that prevented the weeds from growing and taking over. There were three graves. The middle grave was my grandfather's, Jacobs Ozols. On the right side of him was my grandmother, Anna. On his left side was his second wife, Lizete Ozols. We cleaned up what weeds were coming into Lizete's grave and made all three of the graves look well kept. I probably should explain about the graves in European countries. The grave is about six feet in length and has raised concrete sides, about six inches high, all the way around. The middle is filled with soil so it can be planted with flowers or greens. Some plots are bigger than others but most of them are partitioned with a low fence or green fence. Most of the larger plots have a bench where a person can come in and sit to meditate or pray or sit and reminisce. In the summertime, the cemetery looks like a big flower garden. More often than not the cemetery is in a wooded area. I asked Oyars again if we could look for my father's grave but he said it is no longer there. It was destroyed by the "Ruskies" to make room to bury Russian soldiers. I said maybe we could at least find the big headstone down in the woods. We went down to the other end of the cemetery but it was very obvious; there was no trace of anything of my father's grave.

The next place on our list to see in Bauska was the old castle remains. We took a look around the caste ruins just like I did as a small child. Some group was trying to restore the castle ruins, but their progress was slow. The restrooms at the castle remains were a smelly experience. No toilet paper, but on the radiator were 4x4 squares of Manila paper tag board! There were actually feces on the commode. But like in Erfurte, when you have to go, you can make do. Then the men took me to dinner at the café by the castle ruins.

The restaurant is like a bar, but has six tables. The television is playing a VCR tape of a "Ruskie" created X-rated movie. We sat down at the table and the waitress came over and told us what she had on the menu. We can get that or we can go someplace else!

The waitress said, "This is what we have: Latvian salad (made of chopped veggies, egg, canned meat) and a couple of slices of bologna topped with tomatoes and cucumbers and always everything is sprinkled with fresh dill, served with rye bread on the side. To my surprise, it tasted very good. The napkins were ¼ of a full napkin that was cut into fours to make them go a little farther. Oyars and Ainars then took me to see Arvids' house on Uzvaras Street. It looked better than most houses on the outside, because it sits across the street from a "Ruskie" government building built by the Soviets. Even the lawn was mowed on the street side! Oyars said the "big wigs" do not want to look at some shabby old house.

After touring the castle ruins and Arvids' house, it was time to return to Riga and my floating hotel. When I got back to my room, I thought about the day's events. My heart aches for my people, especially in Bauska. The people I saw today were walking around with their faces toward the ground. Their faces showed the cruelty they had endured all of these years. They seldom looked up and never smiled. Most people have to walk to go anywhere; very few have cars. When we were driving in to Bauska in the morning, we saw an elderly lady wearing a dress and a scarf on her head and carrying a basket full of flowers that she hoped to sell at the market. She walked the two or three miles to Bauska. I felt so bad for her but there was nothing I could do. Bauska looks worse than I had imagined. The streets are dirty, the buildings are a shamble and everywhere the grass is overgrown. It reminded me of the slums.

"Please help us!" a man ran up to me with his hands in prayer position, recognizing that I was probably an American by judging my clothing.

"I'd like to, but what can I do? The Russians won't let us bring anything in to this country."

Tears filled my eyes and then I cried for these poor people. I sat on my bed and prayed that God would help the people and lighten their hardships. As I lay down to sleep, my mind was still on the picture of the ancient reverend, pecking at the typewriter with one finger making the documents for me. He sat at his desk with books and papers piled all around him with only the light from one lace covered window. This scene I can never forget.

July 5. Happy Birthday Zachary! One-year old today! He is my second grandson; the first one, Ryan, was born in January. I can't be there, but I sure can think about you all day. As of this writing, Zachary is at Penn State University, main campus, studying dairy science.

Ainars picked me up and took me to his home near Riga but more in the country. I met his wife Dita for the first time, and their two-year old, blond-haired, blue-eyed, little girl Lita. Their son, Andris, I had met a few days earlier. Dita prepared a wonderful meal for us. Oyars and Velta were included in the dinner party. Dita showed me around the two-story house that Ainars built brick by brick. It is by far the nicest house I've seen in Latvia. They have three bedrooms upstairs, and downstairs is a small office that could double as a spare bedroom, but they use it for their computer and the upright piano. Downstairs is a large kitchen with a regular size refrigerator and built-in cupboards. The living room is nicely furnished with an entertainment center against the left wall. The dining room is on the other side of the living room and the dining set is big enough to seat eight people.

July 6. Today a bus was scheduled to tour the Folklore Museum. It is more like an outdoor park than a museum building, except there are no joy rides. But after paying the entrance fee you could walk around the entire park with a map to guide you. Different areas of the park represented different towns in Latvia. I spent most of my time at the Bauska out-door pavilion. Everywhere you went, there were people dancing in their native costumes or singing a cappella, or playing their do-bros, a typical Latvian instrument resembling a guitar but held on the lap and always played by women.

Later that day, I met with Oyars and Velta at the ship and we walked around Riga. Oyars wanted to see what was inside the Dollar Store. Since I was an American I could go in and bring guests. Oyars and I looked around, while Velta got in the checkout line. There was only one! Oyars found something he wanted and by that time Velta was very close to the checkout counter. They know what they are doing! About six o'clock they walked me over to the ancient castle tower by the Daugava River and delivered me to Dagmar. Dagmar is a friend of a friend of my mother. I was to meet with Dagmar and deliver a wig for Dagmar's mother, who had lost her hair from chemo treatments. Dagmar and I took the trolley first, then the shuttle, bus to the amphitheater where a smaller Song Festivals was held. I sat spellbound listening to the voices of combined Latvian choruses from around the world. Men and women, wearing their native costumes, and several thousand strong sing Latvian folk music. The combined orchestra played with the singers. Many solos and different conductors showed their talents to the eager Latvian listeners. It was like an amphitheater, except there was no roof on any part of it. The singers stood on steps that are not only in the front but are also extended to the sides so the singing is stereophonic. The music is so beautiful that I could sit there all night and listen. Just before 11:00 PM we watched the most beautiful sunset go down behind the singers. What a picture in my memory now!

We took the shuttle bus back to the trolley that went back to the ship, and then we parted. Before going in my room, I watched Dagmar walk away into the darkness, and I hoped that she would get home safely. Back in my room, there is still no sign of Janis but I am too exhausted to think about it, and soon I dropped off to sleep land.

July 7. Breakfast was always the same on the ship: bread, bologna, and cold cereal with yogurt. After breakfast, I put on my Latvian costume and went out to the street to meet Oyars, Ainars and Velta. Ainars made his way slowly through the horrendous traffic. Since many of the streets in Riga were closed off for the big parade, it took much longer to get to the parade route and park the car in a safe place. By nine o'clock we were in our observation spot on the street. At ten o'clock the parade came by us. Latvians from all over the world were dressed in their costumes. The leader of each specific group carried a large banner with the name of the group and their city of residence. Some people in the parade did folk dances as they went along but all of them sang Latvian songs to which the crowd could join in too. It was group after group of Latvians and more Latvians. The parade lasted for five hours. It was the biggest and most beautiful parade I had ever seen. Throngs of people filled the streets. Some were in windows and balconies of the buildings on the parade route. I stood there with the bouquet in my hands waving and singing along with the passing groups. I was caught up in this world of Latvian celebration that I did not realize five hours had passed, and I had been on my feet that long! The parade started at the Freedom monument in center city Riga and marched through town to The Daugava Stadium (estrade); about five kilometers. Another exciting day!

After the parade we all went back to Ainars' house where Dita had prepared another delicious meal. As a first course, we had sorrel soup; "skabenes zupa." Sorrel is a green leafy plant that grows wild or can be cultivated. Sorrel grows in the USA too but not too many people know about it or like it. In Latvia, it is a delicacy. She also had fried chicken, mashed potatoes, and gravy. The salad was made of fresh vegetables from the garden diced like a cobb salad. She served a drink called "paninas" very much like buttermilk but thinner and smoother. I didn't want to be rude to my hosts and drank the whole glassful. I regretted doing this much later when my stomach contents started to work through the intestines. For dessert, Dita made a gelatin dessert with fresh berries and a vanilla sauce.

After the evening meal, we went to the Natural Park in Sigulda, which is northeast of Riga. The park has a restaurant, a church, and cement walks all around the park. It is beautifully kept and the grass is cut. Dita and Airars explain a lot about Latvian Folklore about this beautiful, peaceful park. It was a favorite spot for weddings, where the groom may carry his bride down a long line of wide steps. It was also a tradition for the bride and groom and the guests to walk around the park after the wedding.

It had rained before we got here so everything was wet but it did not interfere with us enjoying the park. Suddenly, I felt stomach cramps and I had to make a beeline for the toilette! The toilet room is underground, probably built that way to preserve the park's beauty. It is substandard to what I am used to, smelly and no toilet paper! I always had some of my own with me. I had a difficult time getting my costume pulled up so I didn't soil it. The woolen hand woven skirt of the costume was heavy and bulky making it very difficult to go to the bathroom.

We looked at some shallow caves where people recently and long ago had carved their names or a message. I guess it was not too difficult to carve since it was a sand stone, but carved names and messages lasted forever dated from the 1800's.

When they brought me back to the ship, I was totally, totally exhausted and went right to bed. Still no sign of Janis.

July 8. I spent the morning visiting with Dagmar at their summerhouse outside of Riga. I met her niece, Tina and they served coffee and pastries Latvian style. An elderly man, whom they had cared for until his death, left the little old house to them.

In the afternoon I met Oyars and Ainars at the ship and we were ready to attend the Folk Dance Festival in the estrade. Oyars checked the tickets that I had purchased on the ship, and to our horror discovered that the tickets were for July 6ᵗʰ. I was given the wrong tickets. Ainars was all dressed up in his suit and tie! Disappointed we drove to Oyars' house and watched the dance festival on his TV.

Oyars' wife made supper for us, and then Ainars drove us to the main Folk Song Concert. Arm in arm Oyars and I walked about one kilometer from the drop-off gate to amphitheater. People were here by the thousands. It was estimated that about a total of 100,000 people including the 20,000 performers attended this main event. The concert started at 6:00 PM and we left at 11:00 PM, but the concert was still going on. Oyars said they would probably go on all night. I knew Oyars had to go to work the next day so reluctantly I agreed to leave.

Oyars walked me to the bus that was going to the ship and then got on to make sure I had a seat before he left in the dark of the night. I got back to the ship by 11:45 PM and again the presence of the Ruskie guards reminded me of reality here in Latvia. And still no sign of Janis.

July 9. After breakfast, I got on the tour bus to visit Lutheran Churches, some built in the 1600's, in the western part of Latvia. The tour ended in Kuldiga, my reason for going. The trip without stopping was a four-hour drive from Riga. The bus arrived in Kuldiga at 2:30 PM. Many people had told me that Kuldiga was one of the most beautiful cities in Latvia. My first look at Kuldiga told me this looks just like any other city in Latvia; dirty, gray and fading. The only beauty was in nature. I could see a small waterfall from the bridge when we crossed it and that was beautiful.

By phone Mudeet and I agreed to meet at a certain place, at one of the churches. As soon as I got off the bus, I went to look for Mudeet. She was not in the designated church. Then I went down to the bridge, not there. As I came up from the bridge, I just caught a glimpse of her going into the church looking for me. I ran back to the church quickly and we finally connected.

She is again very upset that the meeting didn't go right. Then she told me of the mix-up. A lady from her church had told her that the tour bus wasn't coming until tomorrow so she went to work. Her husband, Ilmars, just happened to drive through town and noticed the tour bus. No one can miss a tour bus when it comes to town. It is like the biggest happening of the year. Ilmars immediately went to tell Mudeet that the tour bus is here at the church. She ran to the church where I spotted her.

"How long will the bus be here?" I asked the tour leader,

"About an hour," he replied.

Mudeet's husband drove us to their house. The house had been in her husband's family for several generations. Now they were allowed to live in two rooms of the house; the kitchen with only a cook stove and a small sink with cold water, and a multi-purpose room used as a dining room, bedroom and living room The front half of the house was given to another family and a dormer was put in to squeeze in yet another family upstairs. The house was a very old structure and stood among the giant five story apartment buildings built by the Communists on Ilmars' family farmland, and served as apartments for many people who were mostly Russian. The old house has stood time pretty well. The inside is neatly organized but very primitive. The inside rooms were all the same color, yeah, you guessed it—Ruskie green! The paint looks like it was done forty years ago and now looks grubby and dirty. No one was allowed to improve his or her living conditions under the Communist Regime!

Mudeet made a quick lunch of egg salad and rye bread and of course coffee. Then she brought out some pictures. They were pictures of my father, and when I saw them and the gorgeous man that he was, I broke down and cried. I had never seen his picture. I could not remember a face. I was overwhelmed because now I had a face to put with the image of the man I hardly remember. I think if Arnolds Ozols would have lived, he probably would have been much like Oyars; kind, considerate, loving, a true gentleman. The pictures were so precious to me that no money could buy anything that was more valuable to me.

All too quickly, the hour passed and it was time to get back to the bus. Her husband drove us back to the bus but we had plenty of time since the tour was going to see yet another church in Kuldiga. We sat outside the church and talked. Mudite said that her son and daughter and kids had come today to meet me, but she had sent them back because somebody told her, the tour bus was coming tomorrow. I assured her that I would have called if anything changed. And so it goes.

I got back on the bus and Mudeet went back to work. The bus went through Tukums, where we had once so long ago tried to meet up with Millie. The bus did not stop in Tukums, so I took some pictures through the bus window. Since there are no rest stops on any highway, the bus driver stopped the bus on the side of the road in a beautiful wooded area and announced a bathroom break.

"Women on the right side of the road; men on the left," he said.

Either some people did not understand Latvian or couldn't follow directions, since men and women went on both sides! There is no such thing as modesty or privacy here.

Mudeet took the train to Riga and stayed at Alfred's house. The tour bus brought us back to the port, and I went to my cabin exhausted. One of Janis' suitcases has appeared, but still no sign of him. It was end of another day in my Latvia.

July 10. In the morning Mudeet and I went to Jurmala to see the Urpens' farm again. I took many pictures and again had lunch. Then it was time to go back to the ship to meet with Oyars and Ainars. They took me to the auto museum and then to the Brothers' Cemetery. It is comparable to our Arlington Cemetery. Oyars explained what had happened with the cemetery.

"Until about four years ago, no one was allowed in the cemetery because of it being a national shrine. No one was even allowed to go near the cemetery or even leave a flower by the gate. For forty years the cemetery laid in waste becoming overgrown beyond recognition. When Gorbachov came into office, everything changed with his *parastroika* policy. The cemetery was completely cleaned up and people were allowed to go in and visit," he explained.

The cemetery is the final resting place for any dignitaries, soldiers, artists and other Latvian officials. It is so beautiful and serene.

After the cemetery walk, the three of us went to a restaurant. A long line stood outside the doors waiting to go in. Ainars went to the door and immediately was allowed in. He soon re-emerged and motioned for us to come too. We had a wonderful pork chop dinner without bones, *carbonade* to Latvians. After dinner they took me back to the ship.

I sat on my bed and regretted that my time with my family and my Latvia is ebbing to a close. Tomorrow the ship leaves. I packed my suitcases up again taking down the laundry I had done the day before, hanging it all over the bathroom. Janis' other suitcase appeared, but still no sign of him.

July 11. Today the ship leaves Latvia. I have to say goodbye to my homeland, to Riga and to my family. I came here to trace my roots and discovered my heritage. I found my long lost cousins, and most importantly I discovered my father's image. I feel sad and happy at the same time. My emotions are strong and I feel like nobody could ever hurt me again. I had my heritage now.

At the port the whole family had gathered to see me off for home. They all have a bouquet of flowers for me. Mudeet gave me a bouquet of red roses and baby's breath. I had put on my Lord and Taylor dress and white pumps and felt like a queen; Miss America! That is how they made me feel! Then I gave Oyars my "sea bean" and told him that symbolically it means he has to return the bean to me in person. (He returned it to me the very next year when Oyars and Ainars came to the states to visit me.) The sea bean is dark brown and rounded but flat. It is about an inch long and a half inch thick. The family was surprised but pleased to hear the meaning of the bean. Once a bean in my nose; now a bean for Oyars!

It was time to say goodbye. The whole family came to see me off for home. Medeet came from Kuldiga by herself. They all gave me flowers, so my arms were full of them. There were hugs and kisses for everyone. Oyars kissed me on the lips and I gave him a big hug. It was time to leave and as I walked away I said, "So long, until we meet again." They all looked puzzled so I translated it into Latvian for them. Then with a thumping heart, and tears running down my cheeks, I walked off to the passport check. I am filled with love of my father's side of family and the wonderful reunion we had. I will never be the same again. For the last time I went through the passport check and got my passport back and was once more reminded of the ever present "Ruskies" guarding the ship, lest someone should sneak on board and to freedom. Then I boarded the Happy Ship and immediately went up to the deck to get my spot at the railing, even though the ship would not sail for two hours.

Everyone on the ship had flowers and was waving them as we all sang Latvian songs, swaying to and fro, on the ship. The people on the shore were doing the same thing. I threw some kisses to my family gathered on the shore, and they threw some back. As the ship pulled away from the dock everybody sang the Latvian national Anthem, "Dievs Sveti Latviju." Translated into English it says, "God Bless Latvia." When the ship was pulled away from the dock, the guards opened the barricades and let the people flood onto the dock. Some of them followed the Happy Ship down the Daugava shores as far as they could and Oyars did the same. What a send off!

Everyone on the ship was tossing flowers into the river, as did I. Then I tossed one white carnation for Oyars. The last words before distance separated us form the shore was the freedom chant: Freedom we had, freedom will be, Latvia again freedom will see!

Ten Feet From Disaster!

The ship was way up the river and I could no longer see any people on the shore. I stood motionless at the railing gazing at the black silt filled water churning from the propellers. I was in awe trying to digest all that had happened in the last ten days. I did not want to leave the world of wonder that my mind was experiencing. I knew if I looked up, I would see nothing but old rusted battleships sitting still, sitting still as the world moved on.

Suddenly, I was brought out of my deep thoughts by a swift turning of the ship! The ship was edging closer and closer to the shore until the starboard was about ten feet from a wooden plank deck. My immediate fear was that the boat would drift into shallow water and tip on its side. The starboard and the shore were dangerously close.

"Any guess to what is happening," voices on the deck were asking.

"Don't go near the starboard side, or the ship will surely tip over," said another voice.

"Do not fear little flock, for God is with you," came the Bible verse in my mind.

Just moments later, the captain reversed the propellers to get the back end of the ship away from the shore, and once more we were on our way again. The explanation rumor came later. The captain had been drinking and when he saw the boat anchored almost in the middle of the river, and thought the boat was heading right for us. That is when the captain reversed the propellers to avoid hitting the other boat. It turns out that the big cargo ship was anchored in the middle of the river. It was in the same exact place when we came in. I think he should have had his party later. So, he inched his way past the old boat and soon we were on the Baltic Sea again and moving at a great clip. The ship began to sway from one end to the other and I began to get sick.

When Janis and I went to supper (hash browns) I couldn't eat much even though it was very tasty. The ship is now rocking, swinging and swaying as we sped away from my dear Latvia. But I am so exalted that even my upset stomach can't dampen my spirits. Nothing or no one can ever hurt me again.

The captain had a beautiful entertainment program put on for the passengers. I enjoyed it very much, but Janis went to the cabin because there were so seats left and he would have to stand the whole time.

When I lay down on my bed, the room started to go around and around faster and faster. I closed my eyes but it didn't help. Somehow I drifted off to sleep and woke up at 5:00 AM and could tell that we were on quieter waters and I felt much better. I packed up my suitcases and was already to step off the ship. I watched the ship come into the harbor and the workers secure the ship. With suitcases gathered, we slowly got off the ship. I hugged one of the stewardesses and gave her my cabin key. The sailing part of the journey back home was over, but under much better conditions than the first time I was on the Baltic Sea.

Janis and I went back to the same room at Central Hotel. The TV was still not working. I went down to the concierge and complained. At the concierge the man told us that we could move into the executive suite. That dream only lasted a couple of minutes because the man said his boss had reserved it and that he didn't know it. Yeah. Yeah! He apologized and promised to send us a bottle of champagne. By 10:00 PM still no champagne! I called the desk and got some excuse that he was the only one on duty and couldn't bring it. Then Janis went down and demanded the champagne and soon he was back with a small bottle in an ice bucket. Janis poured each of us a glass of the champagne. We each tried it and decided it was the most horrible champagne we had ever tasted! It was sour and bitter at the side time. Yuk! Janis poured it down the sink.

The next morning I went for a walk and heard church bells. I went in and sat down to pray. I gave God thanks for all the wonderful things that I had experienced in Latvia and especially for safety on the journey.

Air France brought us back to Paris where we had lunch, and then onto the Boing 747 to New York City. I have a seat by the window again but being very tired, I dropped off to sleep. When I awoke, I could see nothing but white fluff. We must be above the clouds. We are served supper somewhere over the Atlantic. The flight is so smooth that it feels like I am sitting in my living room, except that it is very crowded. The Boing 747 landed smoothly, and I am back in America.

I now have a chance to reflect on the happenings of the day. I had breakfast in Stockholm, lunch in Paris, supper over the Atlantic and now I'm in New York. Then Janis' crew drove us back to Philadelphia. That's four major cities around the world in one day. Wow!

Janis drove me back to my half-sister's house. I just wanted to talk, but she was so tired, she kept dosing off. In the morning I will have a four-hour drive to get back to Liberty.

Driving home on the North-East Extension of the Turnpike, I had lots of time to think. I reflected once more on the events of the past eleven days. I know I am not the same person as I was before going to Latvia. I have met my relatives on my father's side and they are wonderful. I discovered my roots. I feel so close to my relatives. They radiate so much love and caring. They love me and I love them. I know they will never turn away from me or forsake me. My heart is filled with joy! Then I realized it was Friday the thirteenth, so what! The sojourner returns to Liberty.

I was asked by the Liberty Lutheran Church to speak at a special session one evening. To my surprise, the church was full. My mother sat in the front and kept giving me looks of disapproval. Later she would tell me what I should not have said. Every time I was asked to speak about Latvia, I got the same reaction from my mother. I wondered how I could ever please her. I believed in the Ten Commandments, "Thou shalt honor thy mother and thy father." I just said I am telling the truth that's all. Even with all the disapproval, the sentimental journey was mine and I have relatives that love me.

I made two more trips to Latvia, one in 1994 and again in 2000. They were just as delightful as the first. I could see a distinct difference each time I returned. It was like a Renaissance, an opening of a blossom. Cafes and Bistros had opened all over Riga and flowers were everywhere. The streets were cleaned up. The grass was cut and lots of shops with abundance of products, in Old Riga too. Riga was just like any other city in the world. People were talking on cell phones and were dressed modernly. Unfortunately, not all of my relatives were able to enjoy the abundance as Mudeet passed away in 1997 only two years after her retirement at 62. Oyars passed away in 1998 at age of 70. They both had cancer. I now communicate with their children and grandchildren and Zaiga, the only living cousin left. Selah.

Epilogue

I wrote this book so my children and grandchildren will know something about their heritage. It has been a lifelong dream to write my story, and it became my labor of love. All events are true happenings put in historical perspective. Most people who have read the manuscript have trouble believing that I can remember so much back when I was little. I have pictures and conversations in my mind and I can remember events when I was only two years old. Without this special memory, I would not have been able to write my book.

Unfortunately, the writing of my book has angered some of my family members; therefore I was not able to use their names. They oppose revealing of family secrets, but as I see it the only secret revealed is my own. They even suggested that writing my story is enough; why do I need to publish it? They call it invasion of privacy and are ready to take legal action. I received letters, e-mails and phone messages that were all full of ugly, nasty verbal bombardments. So now I am completely alienated from them; but what else is new?

"The tongue is like a sharp knife; it kills without drawing blood."

—Author unknown

All my life, somebody has censored me, and it continues now. I have finally realized that I cannot do what everybody else wants me to do or write what everybody wants me to write or not write; then I wouldn't have a book at all. It wouldn't be my work. Writing this book has been a wonderful healing process for me and I have enjoyed every minute I spent on the computer, writing, revising, and editing.

Most of my life I have been a loner; going for walks in the woods when I was just a little kid; following animal tracks in the snow; walking in fields of flowers; and picking clover, always on the lookout for a four-leaf-clover. I climbed a mountain in Morris with my two younger kids. I wanted to do it because it is there. And so it is with my story; it has always been there, and now I've had the chance to climb the mountain of *My Heritage, My Destiny.*

978-0-595-46508-8
0-595-46508-0

CPSIA information can be obtained at www.ICGtesting.com
Printed in the USA
BVOW081637200313

316016BV00002B/189/P